FREEHAND
FASHION

CHINELO BALLY

FREEHAND FASHION

LEARN TO SEW THE PERFECT WARDROBE

PAVILION

CONTENTS

ABOUT ME

I am a Nigerian-born Brit with an overly healthy appetite for fashion and sewing. I have always loved fashion, but I began my dressmaking journey just four years ago. After buying my first sewing machine and failing woefully at a couple of attempts at off-piste sewing, I decided to go to my aunty, who is a dressmaker, and watch her in the hope of picking up her magic tricks. Her freehand approach appealed to me because I had many ideas in my head and was itching to bring them to fruition! It took me three months to learn the freehand technique, but I was determined and fell passionately in love with the process of dressing myself this way. The seeds of daring to venture into the fashion industry were – ahem – sown.

I was eager to understand how to make beautiful clothes that fit women of all shapes and sizes and, after only three months of sewing for myself, I began designing and making clothes for family members and friends. I have since made clothes for private clients from all walks of life. In 2014 I took part in the BBC's *The Great British Sewing Bee*, where I learned so much from the judges and my fellow sewists. It was lovely to be surrounded by like-minded people, and to spend so much time sewing!

This is not your conventional sewing book; if you watched the *Sewing Bee*, then you will know that I am not a conventional sewist. This book is all about producing beautiful, elegant and stylish garments using the freehand cutting method. It's aimed at anyone with an interest in dressmaking, and especially the growing numbers of young people who are venturing into sewing for the first time. I want to offer beginners a fresh take on home sewing, one that is fashionable and trendy, and I also want to entice seasoned sewists to step away from traditional rules and try the exciting freehand method. I learned this method without any prior knowledge of sewing; before I appeared on the *Sewing Bee*, I had never used a pattern. This is a technique that everyone can learn, and I look forward to walking you through it, step by step.

ABOUT FREEHAND CUTTING

Freehand cutting is all about marking your measurements directly onto fabric, using simple tools, and developing an understanding of how clothes come together and sit on the contours of the body. It allows you to tailor clothes precisely to your own shape and size – no more fiddling around, adjusting commercial patterns to fit!

Although the idea of freehand garment construction intrigues many in the West, this method has been used traditionally and is still used in many of the less developed parts of the world. Fashion varies greatly around the globe and there is a vast array of traditional dress codes. In Africa and Asia many garments are created, if not entirely freehand, with at least some reference to this approach. I am most familiar with the Nigerian freehand method, and although this has coloured my own sewing technique and style aesthetically, I have further developed what I learned to achieve a high-quality and very precise individual fit, with an exceptional standard of finishing both on the inside and outside of the garments.

My book covers key techniques and the drafting, cutting and construction of five basic blocks and then shows you how to adapt them for different designs. It contains a plethora of exciting projects that range from easy to more challenging. For me, sewing isn't just about craftsmanship, it's also about design; the silhouettes of the garments we will make are timeless, beautiful shapes that have lasted throughout the history of fashion. We will make beautifully fitted gowns for ultra-glamorous events like a posh party or a prom, flattering tops that ooze femininity, and many more garments that will give your wardrobe a facelift.

MY SEWING ESSENTIALS

Nowadays sewing is becoming very hi-tech and gimmicky, but I believe that these new-fangled tools are just candy-coated basics. Before I discovered fancy machine feet, I always did my invisible zips with a standard foot. At one of my workshops recently there was a bit of a panic amongst the students because we only had one concealed zipper foot. I soon calmed them down by inserting the invisible zip with the standard foot. They were dead impressed and I've added a new party trick to my list!

I digress; the point is that although modern equipment makes life easier, it isn't essential. You don't have to be put off doing a buttonhole because you don't have a buttonhole foot; you can carefully use the zigzag stitch on your machine or do it by hand. You don't even need a seam ripper for unpicking your mistakes; just slide a razor blade carefully between the layers and the job is done far quicker.

MY BASIC TOOL KIT

Sewing machine • Iron and ironing board
Tape measure • Small pair of sharp scissors
Large pair of fabric scissors • Razor blade or
seam ripper • Hand sewing needles • Pins
Fabric marker (I use pencil or chalk) • Threads
in different colours to match your fabrics

ALSO USEFUL

Ruler • Overlocker • Pinking shears
Inexpensive poly-cotton fabric for making
templates • Bias binding • Fusible interfacing

TECHNIQUES

I truly believe that, once you've mastered threading your machine and sewing in a reasonably straight line, you can tackle pretty much any sewing project you want! There are a few basic things like neatening seams and understitching that will help to give your work a professional-looking edge, as well as a couple of other techniques that I would urge you to get to grips with. Here are my top techniques for successful stitching!

SEAMS

The majority of seams in this book are very simple – just place the pieces to be joined right sides together and sew, taking the seam allowance specified in the project instructions. There is one slightly more specialised seam that's well worth mastering, and that's a French seam. It's commonly found in shirts, and is particularly useful for sheer or lightweight white fabrics, where you don't want the seam allowance to show through when you're wearing the garment, and for lightweight fabrics that fray easily, as all the raw edges of the seam allowances are enclosed. I've used it in the Easy Chiffon Wrap on page 80.

FRENCH SEAM

1 Place the pieces wrong sides together and sew, taking a 6-mm (¼-in.) seam allowance. Press the seam open and trim the seam allowance to 3 mm (⅛ in.) from the stitching.

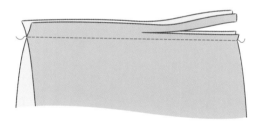

2 Fold the fabric right sides together along the line of stitching that you've just worked. Pin and stitch a second line of stitching, taking a 1-cm (⅜-in.) seam allowance.

3 Press the seam to one side.

SEAM FINISHES

There are several ways to finish seams in a garment. These are just some of them, but I am highlighting them because I use them a lot.

OVERLOCKING

Overlockers are scary machines to those who aren't familiar with them, but once you get the hang of it you won't ever want to be without one. They oversew the edges of the seam with looped stitches to prevent the fabric from fraying; at the same time, two blades trim the seam allowance to reduce the bulk.

Overlocking your seams gives them a shop-bought finish on the inside and keeps you safe from those random stray threads from raw seams. Before overlocking, test the tension with a scrap piece of the same fabric; this is important because you don't want to make any mistakes on the actual garment as the overlocker stitching is less forgiving than the sewing machine's.

You can also use your overlocker to create a rolled hem (see page 14). Each machine will come with instructions for this. If you stretch the fabric as you feed it through you will end up with a beautifully wavy hem, which can add some drama to your garment.

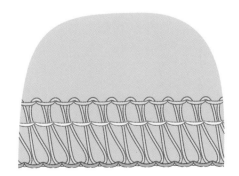

ZIG-ZAGGING

Ziz-zagging your seams is an alternative to overlocking. Like overlocking, this stops the seam fraying, but you will not get the shop-bought finish. The trick to zig-zagging your seams is to make sure that the stitch width is good for the fabric you are using. Test the settings with scraps of the same fabric, and when you are happy with the results trim down your seam allowances to 1.2 cm (½ in.) and ziz-zag them.

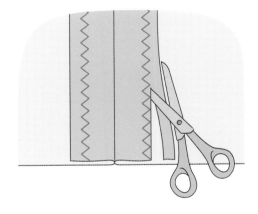

CLIPPING SEAMS

It's important to clip curved seams because failure to do so will result in a puckered neckline or seam line. Clipping gives a seam flexibility, and it is also used to reduce bulk.

To clip a concave curve, make little folds along the seam and cut a wedge out at an angle. Cut away from the stitches to avoid cutting into them. Clip at regular 2.5–4-cm (1–1½-in.) intervals.

To clip a convex curve, simply snip a straight notch into the seam allowance. The notch should just about meet the stitches. This should also be done at regular intervals.

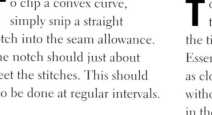

To clip corners, simply cut the seam allowance across the tip of the corner at an angle. Essentially you're trying to get as close to the point as possible without compromising the stitch in the corner.

UNDERSTITCHING

This technique is used to keep the linings and facings from peeking out when the garment is worn; it's particularly important around armholes and necklines. I really do swear by understitching – extreme, I know, but it is so important to understitch any faced edges. I always understitch the seam from the right side of the garment, as I find it easier to keep my row of stitching straight this way, but experiment and see what works best for you.

1 Once you have sewn and trimmed or clipped the seam, spread the pieces out so that the seam is in the middle.

2 With your fingers, press the seam allowance towards the lining or facing.

3 Sew a line of stitching under to the original seam line, no more than 3 mm (⅛ in.) from it. Fold the fabric back along the second line of stitching – the understitching – so that it's right side up, and press. The lining or facing will now sit slightly rolled behind the front of the garment. Press this in place; you should now have a clean, finished edge.

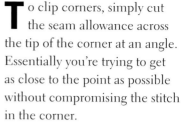

USING BIAS BINDING AS A FACING

This is one of my favourite ways of using bias binding. You can either do this on the wrong side of the fabric so that the bias binding is invisible, or on the right side as a design detail. The great thing with doing this is that you can also blind stitch by hand to give you the cleanness of a bagged-out seam, something I love so much. If you have problems hemming curved seams with perfectly straight stitching, then this will be a great help for you.

My ultimate rule for bias binding is DO NOT PIN; pinning makes it difficult to control as you sew, let your hands do what the pins are supposed to do. For best results, use 1.2-cm (½-in.) bias binding – but never wider than 2 cm (¾ in.), unless you are binding a straight edge.

1 Unfold one side of the bias binding. Right sides together, lay the bias binding on the seam, aligning the raw edges.

2 Working in short sections, keeping the edges aligned as you go, begin sewing along the crease line in the binding. Once the binding is sewn on, clip the seams at regular intervals.

3 Press the binding over to the wrong side of the garment, along the stitching line.

4 Working from the wrong side, sew along the edge of the bias binding to hold it down in place. Alternatively you could blind stitch the bias binding in place by hand.

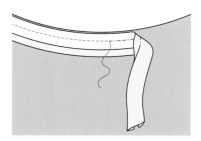

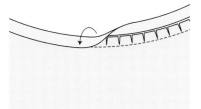

MACHINE-ROLLED HEM

This is my all-time favourite hem. Since learning this style of hem I have hardly used any other sort; I just love the delicate finish it gives to silks, satins, chiffons and cotton. This method of hemming will not work for any thick fabric and you will really need to sew on the edge very neatly, so get a scrap piece of fabric and practise until you are happy with your stitches.

1 Set your stitch length to 1.5 or 2 (you will need a very tight stitch length for this first row of sewing).

2 Turn under a 1.2-cm (½-in.) hem to the wrong side, sewing 3 mm (⅛ in.) from the fold as you turn. Work slowly and keep the hem depth consistent.

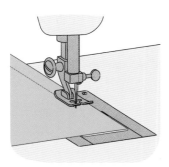

3 Using small, very sharp scissors, cut off the excess fabric as close to the stich line as possible, without cutting into the stitches.

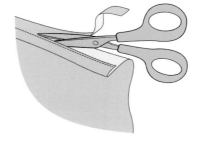

4 Set your stitch length to 2.5 or 3. Turn the hem along the first line of stitching and sew a second line of stitching along the edge, as close as possible to the first line of stitching.

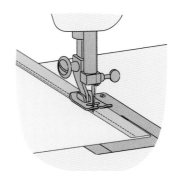

NOTE
I always buy the longest length of invisible zip because you can always cut away the excess when you have finished inserting it. I strongly recommend you get an invisible zipper foot if you're working with a domestic machine.

INSERTING AN INVISIBLE ZIP

There's an abundance of methods when it comes to sewing an invisible zip. I scoured the Internet trying to find one I could understand, because I just couldn't get my head around it. What I learned while sampling other people's instructions was that my aunty was right about not using pins. In fact, when it comes to zips, pins do the exact opposite of what you are using them for. I have taught this method to everyone who has attended my workshops and the general consensus is that it's a lot easier. This is definitely one to throw into your bag of tricks.

1 Following the instructions in your project, stitch the seamed section of the garment below the zip by sewing along your zip-allowance fold from 2.5 cm (1 in.) below the point at which you want your zip to stop.

2 With tailor's chalk, mark your zip stop point (2.5 cm/ 1 in. above the seam you have just sewn) on the right sides of the left and right garment pieces. This is the point at which you stop sewing your zip to the garment, no matter how long your zip is.

3 Lay your garment down right side up and open up the zip allowance folds. Position your zip over the garment right side down. Undo the zip.

4 Take the left side of the zip in your left hand, and the right side in your right hand. The piece in your right hand will be sewn to the left garment piece and vice versa.

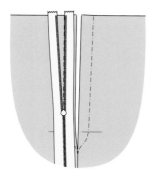

SEWING THE ZIP

5 Attach an invisible zipper foot to your machine.

6 There is always a tiny plastic stop at the top end of an invisible zip; line this up with the top edge of the zip-allowance seam. Position the coils of the zip over the zip-allowance fold, then make sure that the groove in the zipper foot sits directly over the zip coils.

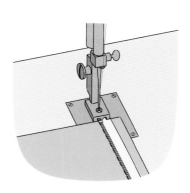

7 Sew your zip in place, making sure that the groove on the foot remains lined up with the zip allowance fold. Be patient with this: it's not a race, so take your time and do it in sections rather than trying to sew the whole zip in one go. I always do a 5-cm (2-in.) section, then I stop, check that I'm lined up, and then carry on. It might sound a little long winded, but it's only a few seconds in practice, and well worth it for saving a few minutes of unpicking. Stop sewing when you get to the zip stop mark. Lock your stitch.

8 Do up the zip. Now using the garment attached to the zip, mark the waist seam (if there is one) and the zip stop point on the back of the side of the zip that hasn't been sewn.

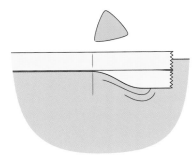

9 Undo the zip again. Match up the zip stop mark on the zip with the zip stop mark on the garment. Pin the second side of the zip in place at this point only. Start sewing the zip from this point, making sure the waist seams/marks on both zip and garment match up.

10 When you get to the top, lock the stitch. Do up the zip to make sure both sides are perfectly matched up.

11 Hand tack the 2.5-cm (1-in.) opening at the base of the zip, then machine sew over the tacking stitches using a standard zipper foot. Turn the garment over, and press the zip allowance folds back; the zip will be almost invisible from the right side.

INSERTING A LAPPED ZIP

With this kind of zip, one side of the zip opening is lapped over the other, concealing the zip teeth. It can be used for the left side of garments such as skirts or for a centre-back opening.

1 Leave an opening in the seam the length of the zip plus 2 cm (¾ in.). Press the seam open, then press the zip allowances to the wrong side.

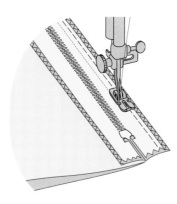

2 Open out the right-hand zip allowance. Place the zip right side down on top, with the teeth running centrally down the seam line. Tack it in place if you wish. Fit a standard zipper foot to your machine, to the right of the needle. Stitch the right-hand size of the zip tape in place, about 6 mm (¼ in.) from the teeth.

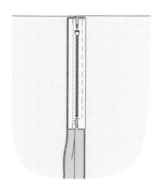

3 Fold the zip allowance back and turn the zip right side up. Position the zipper foot to the left of the needle and stitch along the edge of the fold.

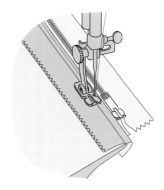

4 Turn the garment wrong side up. Pin and tack the left-hand side of the zip in place.

5 Working from the right side, with the zipper foot to the right of the needle, stitch the zip in place. Start by stitching across the base of the zip, pivoting at the bottom, then stitch up to the top of the zip.

NOTE

You are only stitching the zip to the zip allowance – not to the garment.

TAKING MEASUREMENTS

If you want to use the freehand method, it is important to learn how to take detailed and accurate measurements of yourself. This is the only way you can guarantee that your finished garment will fit you. (A further point to bear in mind is that you may not always have someone handy to take the measurements for you, especially if, like me, you are a bit last-minute.com, always making your clothes on the day you actually need them!) At my workshops I encourage participants to learn how to take their own measurements, but this means making a conscious effort not to distort the body as you do so. If you find it too difficult, then ask someone to help you – and there are some measurements that will definitely require an extra pair of helping hands. I have broken my measuring system in to three groups. There are diagrams to help you on pages 20–21.

HORIZONTAL | These are the measurements that run horizontally across the body. These are the ones that get divided into 2 or 4 in all of the projects.

VERTICAL | These measurements run vertically along the body. They are used as reference points, along which you will mark the corresponding divided horizontal measurement.

OTHER | These are extra measurements that are covered within the projects.

NOTE
Many people wear control underwear under their garments, especially if it's a special occasion. If you will be doing so, it is best to wear it when taking your measurements, because this will affect your proportions and will compromise the fit if not taken into account.

HORIZONTAL MEASUREMENTS

1 Back: from the top corner of one shoulder, straight across to the top corner of the other shoulder
2 Across Back: straight across 2.5 cm (1 in.) above the armpit crease in the back
3 Across Front: straight across 2.5 cm (1 in.) above the armpit crease in the front
4 Bust: around the body at the fullest part of the bust
5 Overbust: around the body at the top of the bust

6 Underbust: around the body at the base of the bust

7 Waist: this refers to the natural waist; a good way to find this is to bend your body to the side – the deepest part of the bend is your natural waist

8 Hip: around the biggest section above the thigh

VERTICAL MEASUREMENTS

9 **Shoulder to Across Back:** from shoulder to 2.5 cm (1 in.) above the back armpit curve

10 **Shoulder to Across Front:** from the shoulder to 2.5 cm (1 in.) above the front armpit curve

11 **Shoulder to Overbust:** shoulder to the point beginning of the bust

12 **Shoulder to Bust:** shoulder to the highest point of the bust

13 **Shoulder to Underbust:** shoulder to the base of the bust, following the contour of the bust

14 **Shoulder to Waist:** shoulder to the natural waist, following the contour of the bust, underbust and down to the waist

15 **Shoulder to Hip:** shoulder to hip, following all the contours of the body

16 **Shoulder to Knee:** shoulder to knee, following all the contours of the body

17 **Shoulder to Floor:** shoulder to the base of the feet

18 **Underarm Length:** base of armpit to desired sleeve length

OTHER MEASUREMENTS

19 **Apex:** across nipple to nipple

20 **Round Sleeve (RS):** around the fullest part at the top of the arm. If you are NOT using stretchy fabric, do not wrap the tape tight because you will need room to manoeuvre

21 **Round Elbow (RE):** as above, but around the elbow

22 **Sleeve Length (SL):** from the top of the shoulder corner to the desired length of the sleeve

23 **Elbow Length (EL):** from the top of the shoulder corner to the elbow

24 **Back Length:** from the nape to the deepest part of the back hollow

25 **Hollow to Dip:** from hollow at base of the neck to desired lowest point of sweetheart neckline

NOTE

When taking measurements from the shoulder down, imagine that you are looking down on yourself from a bird's eye view, and place the head of the tape measure in the very centre of your shoulder.

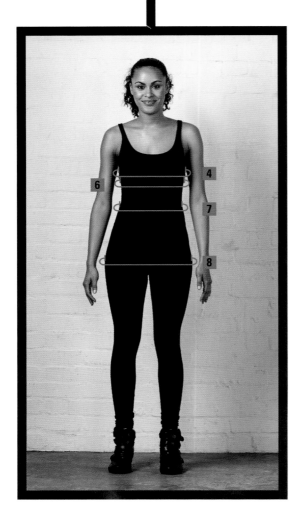
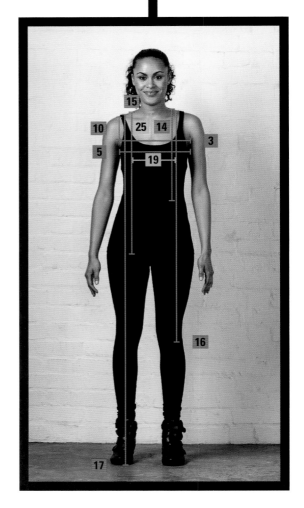

MY MEASUREMENTS

Fill in your measurements on this chart, so that you've always got them to hand.

HORIZONTAL MEASUREMENTS

1 Back ....

2 Across Back ....

3 Across Front ....

4 Bust ....

5 Overbust..

6 Underbust ....

7 Waist ....

8 Hip ....

VERTICAL MEASUREMENTS
9 Shoulder to Across Back......................
10 Shoulder to Across Front ....
11 Shoulder to Overbust ....
12 Shoulder to Bust.................................
13 Shoulder to Underbust.......................
14 Shoulder to Waist ....
15 Shoulder to Hip ....
16 Shoulder to Knee................................
17 Shoulder to Floor ....
18 Underarm Length...............................

OTHER MEASUREMENTS
19 Apex ....
20 Round Sleeve ....
21 Round Elbow ....
22 Sleeve Length ....
23 Elbow Length ....
24 Back Length ....
25 Hollow to Dip....................................

THE BASIC BLOCKS

This chapter covers the drafting, cutting and construction of the basic blocks that are used – either singly or in combination – to make every item of clothing in the wardrobe. There are five basic blocks in my method – bodice, dress, skirt, flare and sleeve.

The **bodice block** is the standard piece that forms the garment from the shoulder seams to the waist seam; it includes princess line darts that give a smooth, body-skimming fit. The **dress block** is for a basic shift dress and contains side bust darts. The **skirt block** can be used as the basis for most skirt styles, from a simple A-line to a figure-hugging pencil skirt. The **flare block** features both the full flare (commonly used to create skater-style dresses or a peplum) and the half flare, which is normally used for maxi skirts and dresses to get a gloriously voluptuous drape around the lower section of the dress. All of these flares can also be used to create ruffles and fancy details in garments. Finally, there is the **sleeve block** – and I have given instructions for a basic fitted cap sleeve, as well as for fuller, puffed and pleated sleeves.

BODICE BLOCK

Conventionally, a bodice block will only address the area covering the shoulders to waist, but with this method we are going to cover the whole torso from the shoulders to the hips.

I will show you how to make a dart best suited for sleeveless garments; I like to refer to this dart as the beginnings of a princess line dart. If you prefer side bust darts, you can use the front darting system in the dress block (see page 34): this will mean that you mark your bust line at 18 cm (7 in.) and follow the armhole steps from the dress block.

NOTES
Always fold fabric right sides
together unless otherwise stated.
It is important to press every
fold to create definite creases.

MEASUREMENTS NEEDED

HORIZONTAL MEASUREMENTS (SEE PAGE 18)
- Back
- Across Front
- Across Back
- Bust
- Underbust
- Waist
- Hip

VERTICAL MEASUREMENTS (SEE PAGE 19)
- Shoulder to Across Front
- Shoulder to Across Back
- Shoulder to Bust
- Shoulder to Underbust
- Shoulder to Waist
- Shoulder to Hip

OTHER MEASUREMENTS (SEE PAGE 19)
- Apex

AMOUNT OF FABRIC NEEDED
- Width = Hip measurement + 35 cm (14 in.)
- Length = Shoulder to Hip measurement + 2.5 cm (1 in.)

EQUIPMENT NEEDED
- Tape measure • Fabric marker • Iron and ironing board • Scissors • Pins

METHOD

1 Fold the fabric in half along the width and lay it flat, smoothing out any wrinkles: this fold is the centre front. Fold over and press a 2.5-cm (1-in.) zip allowance strip right along the opposite edge, folding over both layers of fabric together. This folded edge is the centre back. The top edge is the shoulder seam and the bottom edge is the hem.

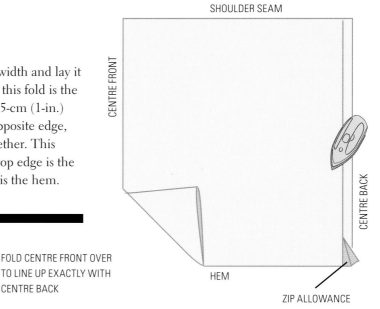

SHOULDER SEAM

CENTRE FRONT

CENTRE BACK

HEM

ZIP ALLOWANCE

SHOULDER SEAM

FOLD CENTRE FRONT OVER TO LINE UP EXACTLY WITH CENTRE BACK

CENTRE FOLDS EDGE

HEM

2 Fold the fabric in half, bringing the centre front over to line up with centre back. Make sure that the edges line up exactly and that all the folds are straight lines.

3 With the head of the tape measure in the middle of the top edge of the folded fabric, use the fabric marker to mark the vertical measurements, adding 1.2 cm (½ in.) to each measurement. Omit your Shoulder to Bust measurement, and instead make a mark at 23 cm (9 in.) for the bust line. The Shoulder to Hip measurement will be the bottom edge, the hem line, of the fabric.

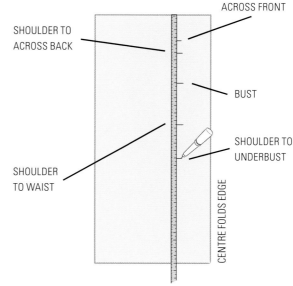

SHOULDER TO ACROSS FRONT

SHOULDER TO ACROSS BACK

BUST

SHOULDER TO UNDERBUST

SHOULDER TO WAIST

CENTRE FOLDS EDGE

4 Visualise these marked vertical measurements as straight lines running horizontally across the fabric; each line has a corresponding horizontal measurement that is measured along it from the centre folds edge. Divide your Across Front measurement by two and add 2.5 cm (1 in.), and mark that measurement with a dot on the Shoulder to Across Front line. Divide your Across Back measurement by two and add 1.2 cm (½ in.), and mark that measurement with a dot on the Shoulder to Across Back line.

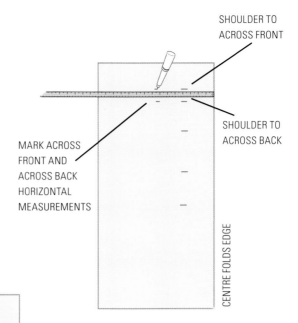

SHOULDER TO ACROSS FRONT

SHOULDER TO ACROSS BACK

MARK ACROSS FRONT AND ACROSS BACK HORIZONTAL MEASUREMENTS

CENTRE FOLDS EDGE

MARK ALL OTHER HORIZONTAL MEASUREMENTS

CENTRE FOLDS EDGE

5 All other horizontal measurements are divided by four and have 5 cm (2 in.) added to them, and are marked along the relevant line with a small cross.

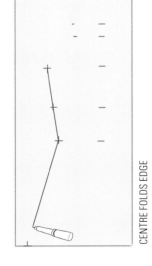

CENTRE FOLDS EDGE

6 Join these crosses with straight lines.

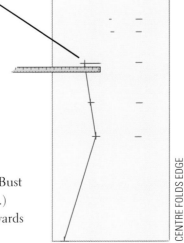

BUST

CENTRE FOLDS EDGE

7 From the cross on the Bust line, draw a 5-cm (2-in.) horizontal straight line towards the centre folds edge.

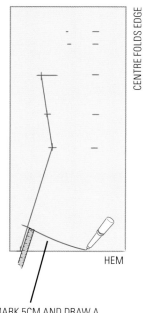

CENTRE FOLDS EDGE

HEM

MARK 5CM AND DRAW A
CURVE DOWN TOWARDS
THE HEM

8 From the cross on the hem line, measure 5 cm (2 in.) up the drawn straight line and make a mark. From that mark, draw a curve that runs down to approximately the middle of the hem line.

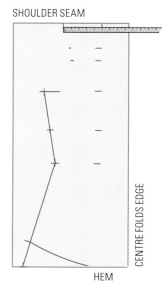

SHOULDER SEAM

MEASURE ALONG
THE SHOULDER
SEAM

CENTRE FOLDS EDGE

HEM

9 Measuring straight out along the shoulder seam (the top edge of the fabric) from the centre folds, make a mark at 9 cm (3½ in.). Divide your back measurement by two and add 1.2 cm (½ in.), and mark that measurement on the shoulder seam.

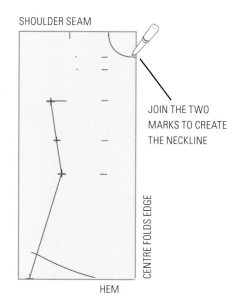

SHOULDER SEAM

JOIN THE TWO
MARKS TO CREATE
THE NECKLINE

CENTRE FOLDS EDGE

HEM

10 Working from the same corner, measure 9 cm (3½ in.) down the centre fold. To create the neckline, draw a scoop that joins the two 9-cm (3½-in.) marks.

11 To create the front armhole, draw a curved line that starts at the second mark along the shoulder seam, touches the Across Front dot, and merges with the end of the 5-cm (2-in.) line drawn at Bust line level. For the back armhole, draw a second line starting at the same point as the first line and following it for 4 cm (1½ in.), but then curving to touch the Across Back dot.

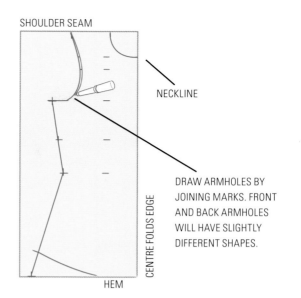

SHOULDER SEAM

NECKLINE

DRAW ARMHOLES BY JOINING MARKS. FRONT AND BACK ARMHOLES WILL HAVE SLIGHTLY DIFFERENT SHAPES.

CENTRE FOLDS EDGE

HEM

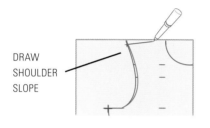

DRAW SHOULDER SLOPE

12 To create the shoulder slope, measure and make a mark 2 cm (¾ in.) down the armhole line. From that mark, draw a diagonal line up to meet the edge of the neckline.

CUT ALONG OUTER ARMHOLE MARKINGS ONLY

13 Cut along the drawn lines through all layers, making sure to cut along only the outer markings in the armhole. Notch the Waist and Underbust levels at the side seams.

MAKE NOTCHES AT WAIST AND UNDERBUST

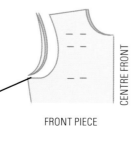

CENTRE FOLDS EDGE

14 Separate the front piece from the back pieces, but keep the front folded in half, and keep the back pieces together. On the front armhole, cut along the remaining drawn line.

ZIP ALLOWANCE

CUT ALONG FRONT ARMHOLE MARKING

CENTRE FRONT

FRONT PIECE

CENTRE BACK

BACK PIECES

MAKING VERTICAL DARTS

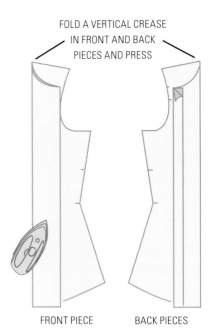

FOLD A VERTICAL CREASE IN FRONT AND BACK PIECES AND PRESS

FRONT PIECE   BACK PIECES

15 Place the folded front piece over the two back pieces, lining up the centre folds. Divide your Apex measurement (see page 18) by two and, from the centre folds, mark that measurement about midway down the length of the bodice. Use this mark as a guide to fold a vertical dart crease running the whole length of the bodice, parallel to the centre folds. Press the fold firmly.

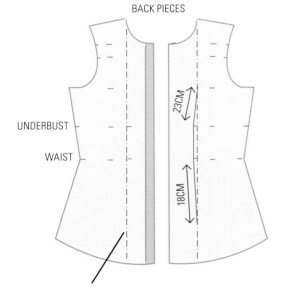

BACK PIECES

UNDERBUST

WAIST

23CM

18CM

DART CREASES SHOULD BE PRESSED TOWARDS THE WRONG SIDE

16 Separate the front and back pieces. All the dart creases need to be towards the wrong side of the fabric, so fold and re-press the lines on the back pieces. Draw the darts to the left of the dart creases (see Note, below) on both the front and backs. On the back pieces, fold the fabric along the vertical dart crease. At the Waist line and Underbust line levels, the dart is 1.2 cm (½ in.) deep, so make marks that distance from the crease and join them with a straight line. Then from Waist line level draw a slanting 18 cm (7 in.) line down to touch the crease, and from Underbust line level draw a slanting 23 cm (9 in.) line up to touch the crease.

NOTE

Why do you always draw the darts to the left of the dart creases? When you stitch the dart, the bulk of the garment will always be to your left, so that it doesn't impinge on your stitching, while the dart fold will be on the very right-hand edge. So the drawn dart line needs to be to the left of the dart fold. If the drawn line is to the right of the fold, it will be on the underside of the fabric and you won't be able to see where to stitch.

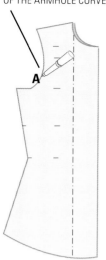

A

17 Working on the front piece, find the deepest part of the curve in the armhole and mark it. (Some sections of the armhole are more of a slightly bent line than a true curve; what you are looking for is the deepest part of the true curve.)

FRONT PIECE

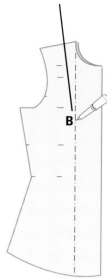

B

18 From the highest point of the shoulder seam, measure and mark your Shoulder to Bust measurement plus 1.2 cm (½ in.) along the dart crease.

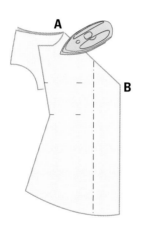

A

B

19 Fold and press what should be a diagonal crease connecting the marks made in Steps 17 (A) and 18 (B).

20 Open out the front piece. All the dart creases need to be towards the wrong side of the fabric, so fold and re-press as needed.

21 The armhole dart is 2.5 cm (1 in.) deep at the edge of the armhole (be aware that the edges may not match up when the dart is folded, but this is fine). Make a mark 2.5 cm (1 in.) from the crease, to the left of the crease line. Draw a 7.5-cm (3-in.) slanting line down from this 2.5-cm (1-in.) mark towards the vertical crease, but stopping 6 mm (¼ in.) short of the crease.

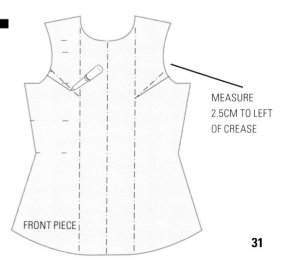

MEASURE
2.5CM TO LEFT
OF CREASE

FRONT PIECE

22 Fold the fabric along the vertical front dart crease. The front section of this dart is 1.2 cm (½ in.) deep at the waist line level. From the waist line level the dart slants down 18 cm (7 in) to the fold, and from the waist up it slants 15 cm (6 in.) to the fold. If you find that the top of this dart is not at least 1.2 cm (½ in.) below the crease interception point, then adjust the dart length until it is.

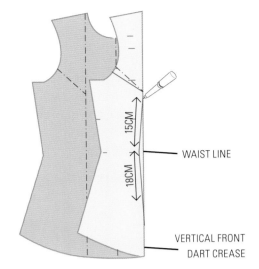

15CM

18CM

WAIST LINE

VERTICAL FRONT DART CREASE

23 You are going to sew this dart as one continuous dart starting from the armhole, but not all sections of the dart will be drawn on the fabric. Start sewing at the armhole, following the 7.5-cm (3-in.) line you drew. When you reach the end of the 7.5-cm (3-in.) line, begin to grade your sewing line down until you are 3 mm (⅛ in.) from the fold. Carry on along the fold until you reach the exact point where the dart creases intercept each other; the easiest way to achieve this is to use the sewing machine handwheel to control the machine manually from 1.2 cm (½ in.) before the interception point, this way you can be very precise. At that point, with the needle down in the fabric, raise the presser foot and pivot the fabric around so that you are now working on the front dart; wriggle the fabric around to release any puckers before putting the presser foot back down. Manually control the machine for a few stitches then continue sewing 3 mm (⅛ in.) from the fold until you come to the drawn dart line. Continue along the drawn dart line until the dart is completely sewn.

SEW AS ONE CONTINUOUS DART

24 Now that you've sewn the dart, there'll be a slight 'step' in the fabric around each armhole. To realign the armholes, fold the front in half and true the curve.

TRIM OFF EXCESS FABRIC TO TRUE THE ARMHOLE CURVE

SIDE SEAMS

25 Pin the back pieces right sides together along the folds of the zip allowance. Lay the back right side up, with the front piece on top, right side down. Make sure that the front centre crease and the pinned zip allowance folds are lined up and that the notches at the side seams are at the same level.

26 Place your hand over the fabric at the Waist line level and grip the side seam with one finger inserted between the layers. Pull on both layers gently so that they are taut and flat. Pin the layers together about 5 cm (2 in.) inside the edges. You may find that the edges don't match up perfectly, and that is fine. Repeat this on the other side, and for both sides at the Underbust line level. Match up and pin the edges at Bust line and hem levels.

27 Starting from the centre crease and working out towards the right-hand side, measure and mark your Bust, Underbust, Waist, and Hip measurements, each divided by four, along the relevant horizontal levels. Join the marks as in Step 6; this line is the seam line.

28 Flip the bodice over so that the back is on top, and copy the seam line you made on the right-hand side. Sew along the lines drawn, and sew the shoulder seam, taking a 1.2-cm (½-in.) seam allowance. Check the fit and make any necessary adjustments. Now your bodice is ready to be assembled. Follow the individual project instructions for details of how to do this.

DRESS BLOCK

Dresses are one of my staples: I love wearing them, and I love making them even more! I experiment a lot with styles, but I tend to favour a classic silhouette. The great thing about this block is that you can play with your very own design ideas and see what you come up with.

MEASUREMENTS NEEDED

HORIZONTAL MEASUREMENTS (SEE PAGE 18)
- Back
- Across Front
- Across Back
- Bust
- Underbust
- Waist
- Hip

VERTICAL MEASUREMENTS (SEE PAGE 19)
- Shoulder to Across Front
- Shoulder to Across Back
- Shoulder to Bust
- Shoulder to Underbust
- Shoulder to Waist
- Shoulder to Hip
- Shoulder to Hem

OTHER MEASUREMENTS (SEE PAGE 19)
- Apex

AMOUNT OF FABRIC NEEDED
- Width = Hip measurement + 35 cm (14 in.)
- Length = Shoulder to Hem + 4 cm (1.5 in.)

EQUIPMENT NEEDED
- Tape measure
- Fabric marker
- Iron and ironing board
- Pins
- Scissors

NOTES
Always fold fabric right sides
together unless otherwise stated.
It is important to press every
fold to create definite creases.

SHOULDER SEAM

MARK THE VERTICAL MEASUREMENTS

CENTRE FOLDS EDGE

HEM

CENTRE FRONT

SHOULDER SEAM

CENTRE BACK

ZIP ALLOWANCE

CENTRE FOLDS EDGE

HEM

METHOD

1 Fold the fabric in half along the width and lay it flat, smoothing out any wrinkles: this fold is centre front. Fold over and press a 2.5-cm (1-in.) zip allowance strip right along the opposite edge, folding over both layers of fabric together. This folded edge is centre back. The top edge is the shoulder seam and the bottom edge is the hem.

2 Fold the fabric in half, bringing the centre front over to line up with the centre back. Make sure that the edges line up exactly and that all the folds are straight lines.

3 With the head of the tape measure against the top edge of the folded fabric, towards the edge opposite the centre front and back folds, use the fabric marker to mark the vertical measurements. Omit your Shoulder to Bust measurement, and instead make a mark at 18 cm (7 in.). Add 1.2 cm (½ in.) to all the other measurements, except for the Shoulder to Across Front measurement, which will be minus 2.5 cm (1 in.), and the Shoulder to Across Back measurement, which will be plus 2.5 cm (1 in.). Omit marking the Shoulder to Hem measurement.

MARK THE HORIZONTAL MEASUREMENTS

SHOULDER SEAM

4 Visualise these marked vertical measurements as straight lines running horizontally across the fabric; each line has a corresponding horizontal measurement that is measured along it from the centre folds edge. Divide your Across Front measurement by two and add 1.2 cm (½ in.), and mark that measurement with a small cross on the Shoulder to Across Front line. Divide your Across Back measurement by two and add 1.2 cm (½ in.), and mark that measurement with a small cross on the Shoulder to Across Back line.

5 All other horizontal measurements are divided by four and have 5 cm (2 in.) added to them, and are marked along the relevant line with a small cross. Along the hem, replicate the measurement you worked out for the Waist line.

SHOULDER SEAM

BUST

WAIST

HIP

CENTRE FOLDS EDGE

HEM

SHOULDER SEAM

CENTRE FOLDS EDGE

HEM

HEM MARK SHOULD BE THE SAME AS WAIST MEASUREMENT

6 Join the crosses with straight lines from the Bust line cross to the Waist line cross. Then from the hem, draw a straight line that stops 23 cm (9 in.) short of the cross at the Hip line. From the Waist line cross, draw a smooth curve that intercepts the Hip line cross and merges with the top of the straight line coming up from the hem.

MEASURE ALONG THE SHOULDER SEAM

7 Measuring straight out along the shoulder seam (the top edge of the fabric) from the centre folds, make a mark at 9 cm (3½ in.). Divide your back measurement by two and add 1.2 cm (½ in.) and mark that measurement on the shoulder seam as well.

8 Working from the same corner, measure 9 cm (3½ in.) down the centre fold. To create the neck line, draw a scoop that joins the two 9-cm (3½-in.) marks.

NECKLINE

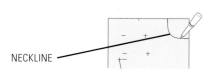

BUST

9 From the cross on the Bust line, draw a 5-cm (2-in.) horizontal straight line towards the centre folds edge.

Freehand Fashion

SHOULDER SEAM

BUST

10 To create the front armhole, draw a curved line that starts at the second mark along the shoulder seam, touches the Across Front cross, and merges with the end of the 5-cm (2-in.) line drawn at Bust line level.

BACK ARMHOLE IS 5CM LONGER THAN FRONT ARMHOLE

11 To create the back armhole, measure down 5 cm (2 in.) from the cross at the Bust line and draw a straight 5cm (2in) line that runs parallel to the 5-cm (2-in.) line above. From the second mark along the shoulder seam, draw a second line that follows the first line for 4 cm (1½ in.), then curves to intercept the Across Back cross, then merges with the straight line just drawn.

DRAW SHOULDER SLOPE

SHOULDER SEAM

12 To create the shoulder slope, measure and make a mark 2 cm (¾ in.) down the armhole line. From that mark, draw a diagonal line up to meet the edge of the neck line.

CUT OUTER ARMHOLE MARKINGS ONLY

UNDERBUST

WAIST

HIP

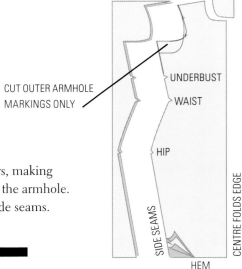

13 Cut along the drawn lines through all layers, making sure to cut along only the outer markings in the armhole. Notch the waist, underbust and hip levels at the side seams.

SIDE SEAMS

CENTRE FOLDS EDGE

HEM

FRONT PIECE   **BACK PIECES**

14 Separate the front from the back pieces, but keep the front folded in half, and keep the back pieces together. Carefully lift the top layer of fabric and, referring to your original markings, redraw the uncut section of the back armhole onto the back pieces and cut out. On the front, cut along the remaining drawn line to cut out the armhole completely.

MAKING DARTS

15 Place the folded front piece over the back pieces, lining up the centre folds. Divide your Apex measurement by two and, from the centre folds, mark that measurement about midway down the length of the dress. Use this mark as a guide to fold a vertical dart crease running the whole length of the dress, parallel to the centre folds. Press the fold firmly.

BACK PIECES

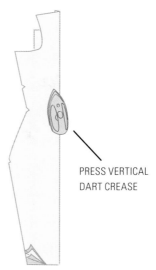

PRESS VERTICAL
DART CREASE

NOTE
Draw the darts to the left of the dart creases on both the front and backs (see page 30).

16 Separate the front and back pieces. All the dart creases need to be towards the wrong side of the fabric, so fold and re-press the lines on the back pieces. On the back pieces, fold the fabric along the vertical dart crease. At the Waist Line and Underbust line levels the dart is 1.2 cm (½ in.) deep, so make marks that distance from the crease and join them with a straight line. Then from Waist line level draw a slanting 18-cm (7-in.) line down to touch the crease, and from Underbust line level draw a slanting 23-cm (9-in.) line up to touch the crease.

BACK PIECES

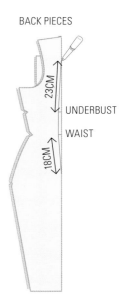

23CM

UNDERBUST

WAIST

18CM

17 On the front piece you need to create side bust dart folds before inverting the creases and drawing the darts. From the Bust line, measure 10 cm (4 in.) down the side seam and mark (A). From the highest point of the shoulder seam, mark the Shoulder to Bust measurement along the vertical dart crease (B).

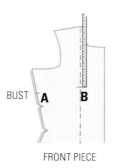

BUST A   B

FRONT PIECE

A   B

18 Fold and press a crease from one mark to the other.

SIDE BUST
DART FOLDS

FRONT
DART FOLDS

19 Open out the front piece. All the dart creases need to be towards the wrong side of the fabric, so fold and re-press as needed. The vertical creases are the front dart folds, and the horizontal creases are the side bust dart folds.

VERTICAL
DART
CREASE

20 Fold the fabric along the vertical front dart crease. The front dart is 1.2 cm (½ in.) deep at Waist and Underbust level. From the Waist line level the dart slants down 18 cm (7 in.) to the fold. Also from the Waist line level, measure 15 cm (6 in.) up to the fold, but draw the slanted line from Underbust level, as shown.

21 Fold the fabric along the side bust dart crease. Measure up 2.5 cm (1 in.) along the armhole; this is the depth of the dart. Measure 4 cm (1½ in.) along the crease, and make a mark 2.5 cm (1 in.) up from that point. Join the two marks with a straight line, then draw a 10-cm (4-in.) line that slants down to the fold.

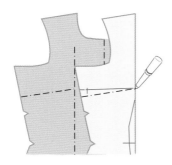

PRESS SIDE
DARTS DOWN

PRESS
VERTICAL
DARTS
OUTWARDS

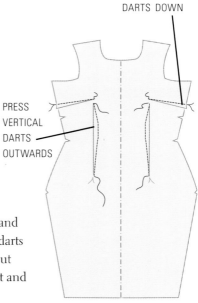

22 Sew the darts in the front and back pieces and press the darts outwards. Be careful not to press out the centre creases in both the front and the back pieces.

SIDE SEAMS

23 Pin the back pieces right sides together along the folds of the zip allowance. Open out the pinned back piece and lay it right side up on your work surface, with the front piece on top, right side down. Make sure that the front centre crease and the pinned zip allowance folds are lined up and that the notches at the side seams are at the same level.

24 Place your hand over the fabric at the Waist line level and grip the side seam with one finger inserted between the layers. Pull on both layers gently so that they are taut and flat. Pin the layers together about 5 cm (2 in.) inside the edges. You may find that the edges don't match up perfectly, and that is fine. Repeat this on the other side, and for both sides at the Underbust line level. Match up and pin the edges at Bust line and Hem line levels.

25 Starting from the centre crease and working out towards the right-hand side, measure and mark your Bust, Underbust, Waist, and Hip measurements, each divided by four, along the relevant horizontal levels. Join the marks as in Step 6; this line is the seam line.

26 Flip the bodice over so that the back is on top, and copy the seam line you made on the right-hand side. Sew along the lines drawn, and sew the shoulder seam, taking 1.2-cm (½-in.) seam allowances. Check the fit and make any necessary adjustments. Now your dress is ready to be assembled. Follow the individual project instructions for details of how to do this.

SKIRT BLOCK

Skirts are must-haves for me because I love the idea of separates and enjoy mixing and matching my wardrobe, but I know that this isn't the case for every woman. This block doesn't just offer you the base for most skirt styles; it can also be added to a waist-length version of the bodice block (see page 24) to create dresses with a waist seam. I have quite a deep hollow in my back and I find that fitting around the waist is a problem when I wear skirts that are shop-bought. If, like me, this is your plight, make the back darts 2 cm (¾ in.) deep at waist level rather than the 1.2 cm (½ in.) suggested; this will make the skirt hug your curves better.

NOTES

Always fold fabric right sides
together unless otherwise stated.
It is important to press every fold
to create definite creases.

MEASUREMENTS NEEDED

HORIZONTAL MEASUREMENTS (SEE PAGE 18)
- Waist
- Hip

VERTICAL MEASUREMENTS (SEE PAGE 19)
- Waist to Hip
- Waist to Knee

AMOUNT OF FABRIC NEEDED
- Width = Hip measurement + 35.5 cm (14 in.)
- Length = Waist to Knee measurement + 2.5 cm (1 in.)

EQUIPMENT NEEDED
- Tape measure
- Fabric marker
- Iron and ironing board
- Pins
- Scissors

METHOD

1 Fold the fabric in half along the width and lay it flat, smoothing out any wrinkles: this fold is centre front. Fold over and press a 5-cm (2-in.) zip allowance strip right along the opposite edge, folding over both layers of fabric together. This folded edge is centre back.

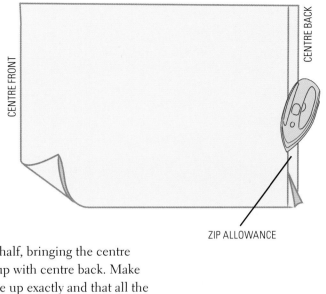

CENTRE FRONT

CENTRE BACK

ZIP ALLOWANCE

CENTRE FRONT   CENTRE BACK

2 Fold the fabric in half, bringing the centre front over to line up with centre back. Make sure that the edges line up exactly and that all the folds are straight lines, or the final hem line will be uneven. Press the folds.

CENTRE FOLDS
SHOULD LINE UP

3 With the head of the tape measure on the top edge of the folded fabric, use the fabric marker to mark the vertical measurements: mark your Waist to Hip measurement plus 1.2 cm (½ in.), and your Waist to Knee measurement plus 2.5 cm (1 in.), with small dashes. The top edge of the fabric is now the Waist line, the first dash is the Hip line, and the lowest dash, which should be on the bottom edge of the fabric, is the Hem line.

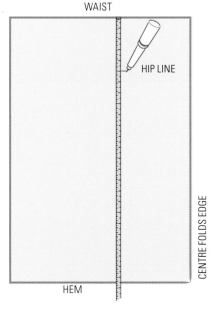

WAIST

HIP LINE

CENTRE FOLDS EDGE

HEM

4 Visualise these marked vertical measurements as straight lines running horizontally across the fabric; each line has a corresponding horizontal measurement that is measured along it from the centre folds edge. Divide your Waist measurement by four and add 5 cm/ 2 in. (add 7.5 cm/3 in. if you are a curvier lady), and mark that measurement along the waist line with a small cross.

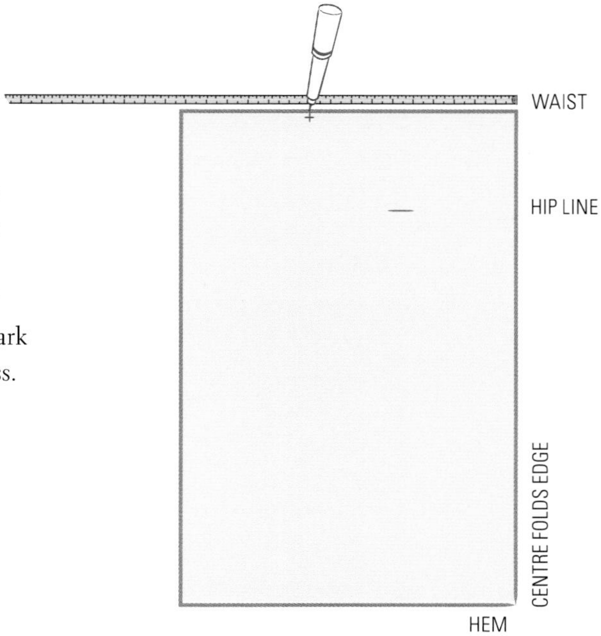

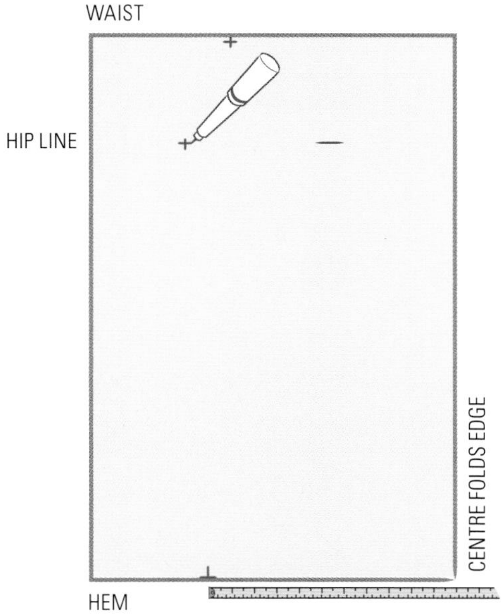

WAIST

HIP LINE

CENTRE FOLDS EDGE

HEM

WAIST

HIP LINE

CENTRE FOLDS EDGE

HEM

5 Divide your Hip measurement by four and add 5 cm/2 in. (or 7.5 cm/3 in., as in Step 4), and mark that measurement along the Hip line with a small cross. Deduct 2.5 cm (1 in.) from the Hip line measurement, and mark that new measurement along the Hem line.

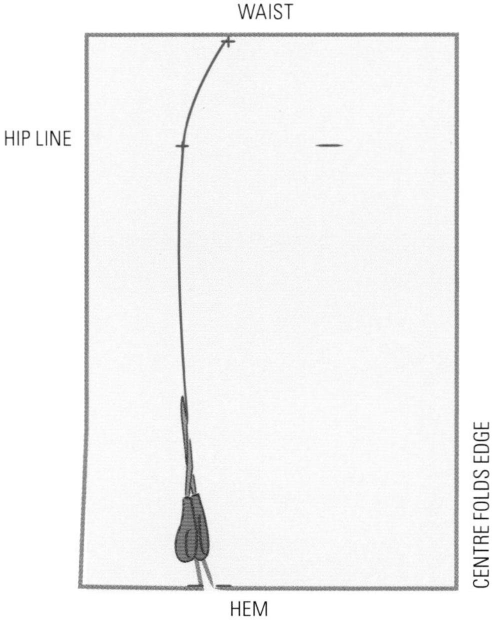

WAIST

HIP LINE

CENTRE FOLDS EDGE

6 Join the crosses with a smooth, curving drawn line: this is the side seam line. Cut along this line, cutting through both layers.

HEM

7 Separate the skirt front, the top piece of folded fabric, from the skirt backs. On the centre front fold, measure down 1.2 cm (½ in.) from the Waist line and make a mark. Draw a curved line that slopes upwards from this mark to the side seam at the Waist line. Cut along this line.

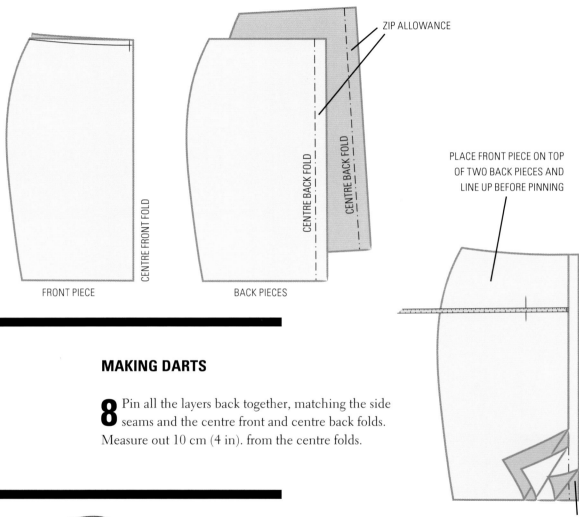

FRONT PIECE

CENTRE FRONT FOLD

BACK PIECES

CENTRE BACK FOLD

CENTRE BACK FOLD

ZIP ALLOWANCE

PLACE FRONT PIECE ON TOP
OF TWO BACK PIECES AND
LINE UP BEFORE PINNING

ZIP ALLOWANCE

MAKING DARTS

8 Pin all the layers back together, matching the side seams and the centre front and centre back folds. Measure out 10 cm (4 in). from the centre folds.

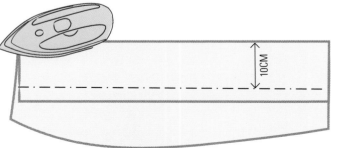

10CM

9 Fold the fabric at the 10-cm (4-in.) measurement, making sure that the fold is parallel to the centre front and centre back folds. This crease will be the centre line of each dart, so press it firmly.

10 Separate all the pieces and unfold them. Two of the dart creases will be towards the right side of the fabric, and the other two towards the wrong side. All the dart folds need to be creased towards the wrong side of the fabric, so fold and re-press lines as needed.

RE-PRESS SO ALL DART FOLDS ARE CREASED TOWARDS THE WRONG SIDE

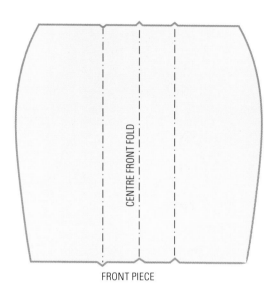

CENTRE FRONT FOLD

FRONT PIECE

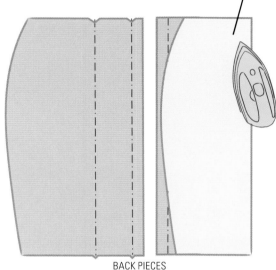

BACK PIECES

DRAW DARTS ON LEFT SIDE OF DART CREASE

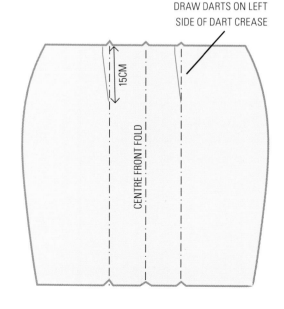

15CM

CENTRE FRONT FOLD

11 Draw the darts to the left of the dart creases on the front and back pieces. The darts on this skirt should be 1.2 cm (½ in.) deep at the waist (or 2.5 cm/1 in. deep if you added 7.5 cm/ 3 in. to the Waist and Hip measurements in Steps 4 and 5), and 15cm (6in) long. Now your skirt is ready to be assembled. Follow the individual project instructions for details of how to do this.

FLARE BLOCK

A flare is a circle or a section of a circle, and is used to create skirts (see pages 66 and 102) and peplums (see page 118). Following are the calculations and fabric arrangement for two flare blocks: the flare and the full flare. These blocks can create dramatic drapes, depending on the fullness you decide on and the length involved. The difference in creating the two blocks lies in the fabric arrangement and the division formula.

MEASUREMENTS NEEDED

- Waist (see page 18)
- Flare length (see below)

FORMULA

- Flare (half-circle) formula: waist measurement ÷ 3.14
- Full flare (full circle) formula: waist measurement ÷ by 3.14 ÷ 2

AMOUNT OF FABRIC NEEDED

Firstly, work out your chosen formula. You will always end up with a decimal number; round that down to the nearest whole or half number, and that is your first radius. This will be the waist of the garment.

Secondly, work out the flare length. For example, if you are making a dress with a flared skirt, work out the flare length by subtracting your Shoulder to waist measurement from your Shoulder to hem measurement, then adding 4 cm (1½ in.).

Add the flare length to your first radius, and that number is your second radius. This will be the hem of the garment.

FABRIC FOR A FLARE

Width = second radius x 2
Length = second radius + 2.5 cm (1 in.)

FABRIC FOR A FULL FLARE

Width = second radius x 2 + 2.5 cm (1 in.)
Length = second radius x 2 + 2.5 cm (1 in.)

EQUIPMENT NEEDED

- Tape measure
- Fabric marker
- Iron and ironing board
- Scissors

NOTES

Always fold fabric right sides together unless otherwise stated. It is important to press every fold to create definite creases. Both cuts can have allowances for centre-back zips, if wanted. If a zip isn't needed, then simply leave those edges unfolded and follow the steps, lining up the centre front fold with the edges of the fabric instead of with the edges of the zip allowance folds.

METHOD FOR FLARE

1 Fold the fabric in half along the width and lay it flat, smoothing out any wrinkles: this fold is centre front. With the centre front fold at the top as you look at it, designate the right-hand edge of the folded fabric as centre back. Fold over and press a 2.5-cm (1-in.) zip allowance strip right along the centre back (if a centre back zip is required), folding over both layers of fabric together.

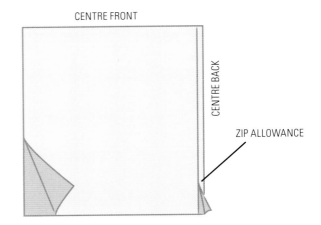

CENTRE FRONT

CENTRE BACK

ZIP ALLOWANCE

2 Bring the centre front folded edge over to line up with the folded edge of the zip allowance. The resulting bias fold will be the side seams. It is very important that the centre front fold lines up exactly with the zip allowance fold, and that the top corner is a sharp point, but don't worry if the bottom edges don't align. Make sure that all the folds are straight lines, or the final hem line will be uneven. Press the folds.

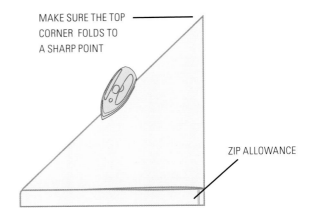

MAKE SURE THE TOP CORNER FOLDS TO A SHARP POINT

ZIP ALLOWANCE

3 Positioning the head of the tape on the point, pivot and use the fabric marker to mark the first radius, and then the second radius.

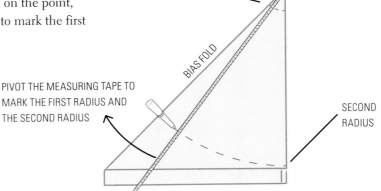

FIRST RADIUS

BIAS FOLD

PIVOT THE MEASURING TAPE TO MARK THE FIRST RADIUS AND THE SECOND RADIUS

SECOND RADIUS

4 Cut along the marked radius lines, cutting through all layers. Cut along the bias fold, cutting through both layers of fabric.

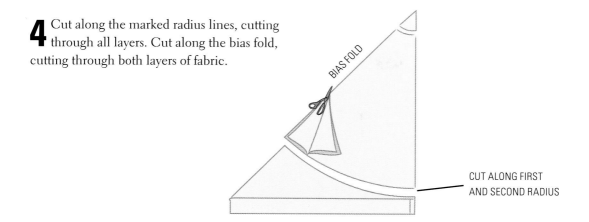

BIAS FOLD

CUT ALONG FIRST
AND SECOND RADIUS

5 The resulting pieces are one front with a pressed centre front fold, and two backs, with pressed zip allowances. Now your flare is ready to be assembled. Follow the individual project instructions for details of how to do this.

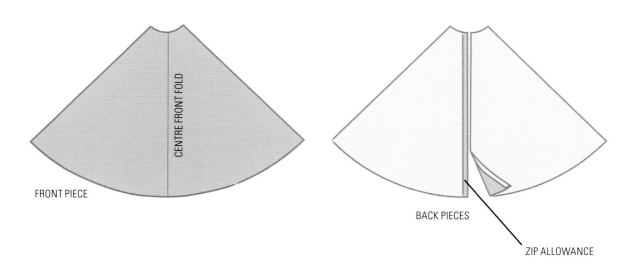

CENTRE FRONT FOLD

FRONT PIECE

BACK PIECES

ZIP ALLOWANCE

METHOD FOR FULL FLARE

This full-circle cut can be made with side seams and a centre back zip allowance, or with no seams at all.

NO SEAMS

1 Fold the fabric in half lengthways and in half again widthways. The folds need to be very precise; press them at each stage.

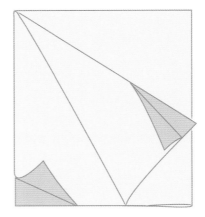

2 From the corner where all the folded edges meet, pivot and use the fabric marker to mark the first radius, and then the second radius.

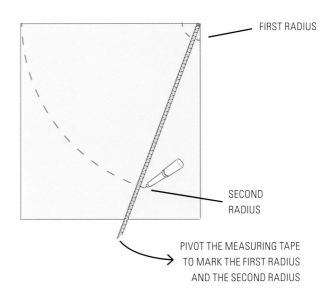

FIRST RADIUS

SECOND RADIUS

PIVOT THE MEASURING TAPE TO MARK THE FIRST RADIUS AND THE SECOND RADIUS

3 Cut along the marked lines and unfold the complete circle.

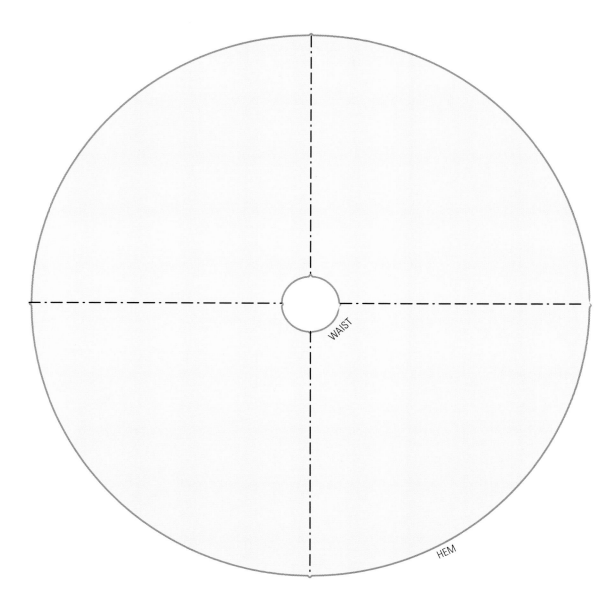

WAIST

HEM

WITH SIDE SEAMS AND ZIP ALLOWANCE

1 Fold the fabric in half along the width and lay it flat, smoothing out any wrinkles: this fold is centre front on the front piece, and the side seams on the back pieces. With this fold at the top as you look at it, designate the right-hand edge of the folded fabric as centre back. Fold over and press a 2.5-cm (1-in.) zip allowance right along centre back (if a centre back zip is required), folding over both layers of fabric together.

CENTRE FRONT ON FRONT (SIDE SEAMS ON BACK)

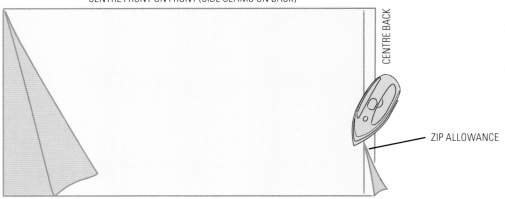

CENTRE BACK

ZIP ALLOWANCE

2 Fold the fabric in half, bringing the edge opposite the zip allowance over to line up with the folded edge of the zip allowance. Make sure that the edges line up exactly and that all the folds are straight lines, or the final hem line will be uneven. Press the folds.

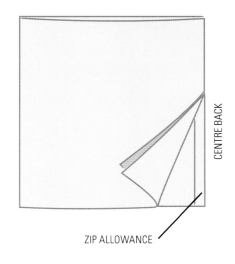

CENTRE BACK

ZIP ALLOWANCE

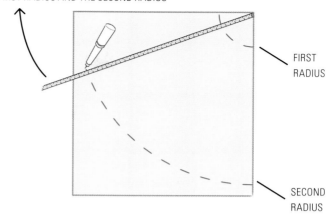

PIVOT THE MEASURING TAPE TO MARK THE FIRST RADIUS AND THE SECOND RADIUS

3 Positioning the head of the tape on the corner lying on top of the folded edge of the zip allowance, pivot and use the fabric marker to mark the first radius, and then the second radius.

FIRST RADIUS

SECOND RADIUS

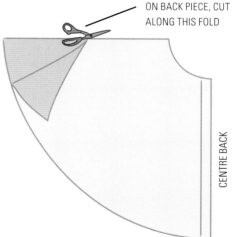

ON BACK PIECE, CUT ALONG THIS FOLD

4 Cut along the marked radius lines, cutting through all layers. On the back piece (the piece with the zip allowance), cut along the fold opposite the zip allowance to establish the side seams.

CENTRE BACK

5 The resulting pieces are one front with a pressed centre front fold, and two backs, with pressed zip allowances. Now your flare is ready to be assembled. Follow the individual project instructions for details of how to do this.

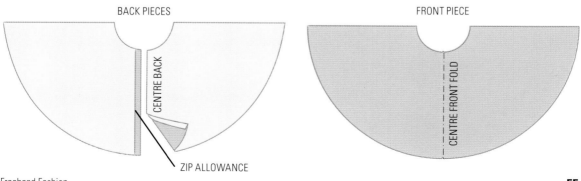

BACK PIECES

FRONT PIECE

CENTRE BACK

ZIP ALLOWANCE

CENTRE FRONT FOLD

SLEEVE BLOCK

Sleeves are one of those things that even experienced sewists really fear. When I first started sewing, everything I made was sleeveless, which was unfortunate because I really don't like showing my arms. The freehand approach to sleeves does not involve any complicated maths for working out the sleeve head, but it will take some practice before your mind registers what the right curve looks like. I suggest making up a bodice block out of an inexpensive poly-cotton (abundantly available in markets and fabric shops everywhere), in order to practise cutting and setting in your sleeves until you have grown confident. I'll let you in on a little secret: I did this for an entire day and really learnt a lot about sleeves.

NOTES

Always fold fabric right sides together unless otherwise stated. It is important to press every fold to create definite creases.

MEASUREMENTS NEEDED

HORIZONTAL MEASUREMENTS (SEE PAGE 18)

- Round Sleeve
- Round Elbow
- Wrist

VERTICAL MEASUREMENTS (SEE PAGE 19)

- Sleeve Length
- Underarm Length
- Elbow Length

AMOUNT OF FABRIC NEEDED

- Width = Round Sleeve x 2 + 5 cm (2 in.)
- Length = Sleeve Length + 4 cm (1½ in.)

EQUIPMENT NEEDED

- Tape measure
- Fabric marker
- Iron and ironing board
- Metre rule
- Scissors

NOTES

This section will show you how to cut a sleeve with a fitted cap, and a puff sleeve. Note that you are making two sleeves at the same time.

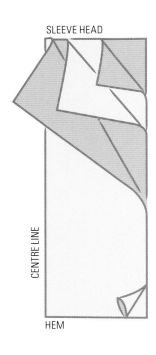

SLEEVE HEAD

CENTRE LINE

HEM

METHOD

1 Fold the fabric in half along the width and then in half along the width again. The top edge is the sleeve head, the bottom edge is the hem, and the side with the second fold is the centre line of the sleeve.

2 Subtract your Underarm Length from your Sleeve Length; the result is your sleeve cap height. Place the head of the tape measure on the sleeve head edge and use the fabric marker to mark your sleeve cap height and elbow length.

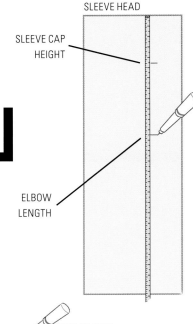

SLEEVE HEAD

SLEEVE CAP HEIGHT

ELBOW LENGTH

3 Visualise these marked vertical measurements as straight lines running horizontally across the fabric; each line has a corresponding horizontal measurement that is measured along it from the centre line edge. Divide your Round Sleeve measurement by two and add 1.2 cm (½ in.), and mark that measurement with a cross on the sleeve cap height line. Divide your Round Elbow measurement by two and add 1.2 cm (½ in.), and mark that measurement with a cross on the Elbow Length line. Divide your Wrist measurement by two and add 1.2 cm (½ in.), and mark that measurement with a cross on the hem.

SLEEVE CAP HEIGHT —

ELBOW LENGTH —

WRIST

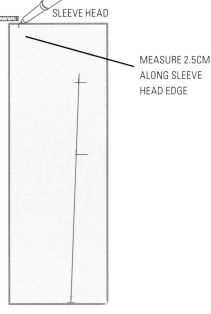

SLEEVE HEAD

MEASURE 2.5CM ALONG SLEEVE HEAD EDGE

4 Using the rule, join the crosses with a straight line. From the top of the centre line edge, measure and mark 2.5 cm (1 in.) along the sleeve head edge.

5 This is the part of the sleeve that requires practice to get the curves right. From the cross on the sleeve cap line, draw a concave slope up to about one-third of the way towards the sleeve head.

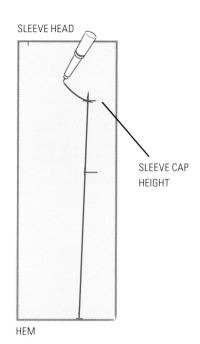

SLEEVE HEAD

SLEEVE CAP HEIGHT

HEM

ROUND OFF THE LINE AT
THE SLEEVE HEAD EDGE

6 Continue the curve upwards as shown, rounding off into the mark on the sleeve head edge.

MAKE A NOTCH
AT THE CENTRE OF
THE SLEEVE HEAD

7 Cut along the drawn lines through all layers to cut out two sleeves. Notch the centre lines at the sleeve head, and the elbow length on the side seams.

MAKE A NOTCH
AT THE ELBOW

SETTING IN THE SLEEVES

For all sleeves, I always find it easiest to have the sleeve right side out and the garment wrong side out. I then insert the sleeve into the garment armhole so that the right side of the sleeve is facing the right side of the garment, but I am working from the wrong side of both.

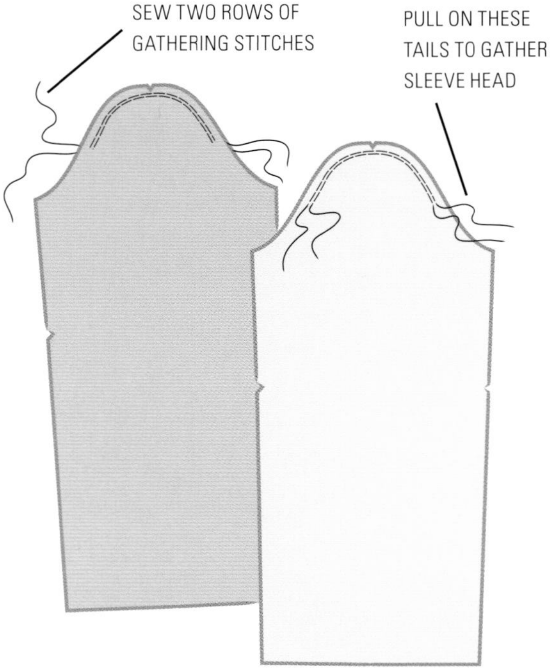

SEW TWO ROWS OF
GATHERING STITCHES

PULL ON THESE
TAILS TO GATHER
SLEEVE HEAD

STANDARD FITTED SLEEVE HEAD

1 Sew two rows of long-length stitches (gathering stitch) along the sleeve head, close together and 6 mm (¼ in.) and 1 cm (⅜ in.) from the edge. Start and end each row 4 cm (1½ in.) from the sleeve side seam, and leave a tail of thread at the beginning and end of each row.

2 Pull gently on the tails to very slightly gather the sleeve head.

3 Sew the side and shoulder seams of the garment, taking a 1.2-cm (½-in.) seam allowance. Sew the sleeve underarm seams, neaten the seam allowances and press the seams open. Turn the sleeves right side out.

4 Right sides together, slip the sleeve into the bodice. Match up the side seam of the sleeve with the side seam of the bodice and pin the layers together. Pin the centre line notch in the sleeve to the shoulder seam of the bodice. Ease the sleeve head to fit into the armhole by adjusting the gathering stitches, making sure the fullness is equally spread across the sleeve head and pin in place all the way around.

THE NOTCH IN THE CENTRE OF THE SLEEVE HEAD SHOULD LINE UP WITH THE SHOULDER SEAM

THE SIDE SEAM OF THE SLEEVE SHOULD MATCH UP WITH THE SIDE SEAM OF THE GARMENT

GARMENT IS WS OUT, AND SLEEVE IS RS OUT

5 Starting from the side seam, sew the sleeve in place. Alternatively you can tack the sleeve in place and then machine sew it, removing the tacking stitches afterwards.

EXTEND YOUR SLEEVE CAP HEIGHT AS REQUIRED

TO MAKE A PUFFED OR PLEATED SLEEVE

The fabric length needs to be at least 13cm (5in) longer than the sleeve length (experiment with different lengths for different sleeve head heights).

1 Subtract your Underarm Length from your Sleeve Length; the result is your sleeve cap height. Add the extra length to this measurement and this is the new sleeve cap height. Using this measurement, draft the sleeve following the standard method.

PUFFED SLEEVE

1 Gather the sleeve as for a standard fitted sleeve, but pulling up the gathers more tightly. Pin the sleeve into the bodice at the side seam and shoulder seam as for a standard fitted sleeve, and make sure the gathers are evenly distributed. Sew the sleeve in place.

INCREASING THE SLEEVE CAP HEIGHT CREATES THE PUFFED EFFECT

MAKE
NOTCHES

PLEATED SLEEVE

1 In the armhole of the bodice, snip small notches at the beginning and end of the area you want the pleats to be. Pin the sleeve into the bodice at the side seam and shoulder seam, as for a standard fitted sleeve.

2 Starting from the side seam, sew the sleeve up to the notch in the bodice armhole on both sides.

3 Measure the unsewn section of the sleeve and the unsewn section of the armhole. Subtract the latter measurement from the former. Divide the result by the desired depth of the pleats: this will tell you how many pleats you will get. If this gives you a decimal number, round it to the nearest whole number.

SEW UP TO
NOTCHES

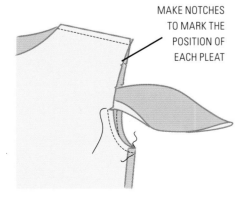

MAKE NOTCHES
TO MARK THE
POSITION OF
EACH PLEAT

4 In the bodice armhole, make notches at the desired position of each pleat. For example, if there are to be six pleats (or three on each side), then make three evenly spaced notches on either side of the shoulder seam. If you end up with an odd number like 7, then you will have a pleat in the shoulder seam; this pleat will be a box pleat (see step 7).

5 Decide which direction you want your pleat to go – remember that they must go in the same direction on either side of the shoulder seam. Here the pleats are 5 cm (2 in.) deep, so I made a tuck that measures 2.5 cm (1 in.) on either side at each notch. Make your first pleat at the first notch.

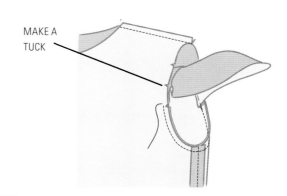

MAKE A TUCK

6 Form the rest of the pleats, omitting the one at the shoulder seam if you have an odd number of pleats.

PIN THE PLEATS IN PLACE

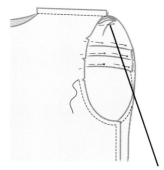

FORM A BOX PLEAT

7 If you have an odd number of pleats, use the excess fabric at the head of the sleeve to create a box pleat.

8 Sew the rest of the sleeve in place.

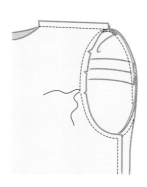

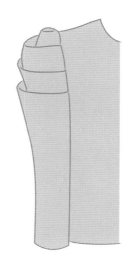

THE
PROJECTS

H ere you will find tops, skirts, dresses and jackets that I have designed to walk you through the freehand cutting method. If you are used to sewing with patterns, you may find this a bit tricky to get your head around at first, but trust me, it's easy when you know how! The simpler projects are at the start, followed by the more challenging ones. As you work through the garments you will pick up skills that will aid you as the tasks become more intense. For some items I have made two versions, to show you the different effects that can be achieved by choosing different fabric and making small design adjustments. As you grow in confidence you will want to experiment, making the clothes that you've always had in mind but couldn't find in the shops. I want to encourage you to try unusual fabrics and embellishments to make the clothes suit your own style. I want to free you from the restrictions of commercial sewing patterns and inspire you to bring to life your own fashions. I warn you: you may never want to buy ready-made clothes again!

MAXI
SKIRT

For me, nothing beats a romantic look in the summer, and what's more romantic than a beautifully floaty maxi skirt. This one is an absolute winner with all body shapes because it hugs closely at the waist then flares out skimming the rest of the lower torso and legs. The great thing about this cut is its versatility; you can use all kinds of fabrics and achieve very different looks. A stiffer cotton fabric will fall with more structure and lend itself to a fuller silhouette, whilst a soft silk-satin will give you a deliciously liquid drape. If you don't fancy the full-length version, just make it shorter. Remember, you are the designer, so play with fabrics, lengths, embellishments; let your imagination run free.

MEASUREMENTS NEEDED

Waist • First radius (see page 49)
Second radius (see page 49)

BLOCK NEEDED

Flare Block (see page 48)

AMOUNT OF FABRIC NEEDED

Width = second radius x 2 + 91.5 cm (1 yd)
Length = fabric that measures at least 145 cm (58 in.)
across from selvedge to selvedge

EQUIPMENT NEEDED

Fabric • Fusible interfacing • Straight ruler
Tape measure • Fabric marker
Iron and ironing board • Sewing machine
Sewing thread to match fabric
Invisible zip • Fabric scissors

NOTES

Always fold fabric right sides together unless otherwise stated. It is important to press every fold to create definite creases. Take a 1.2-cm (½-in.) seam allowance throughout unless otherwise stated.

1 Follow the instructions for the flare block to work out the first radius. The second radius will be the desired skirt length plus 4 cm (1½ in.) plus the first radius. Multiply the second radius by two and measure that length along the selvedge of the fabric and cut off the excess. Set the excess aside.

2 Fold the fabric in half along the selvedge; this is the centre front fold. Follow steps 1–5 of the method for a flare from the Flare Block, folding over the 2.5-cm (1-in.) zip allowance at centre back.

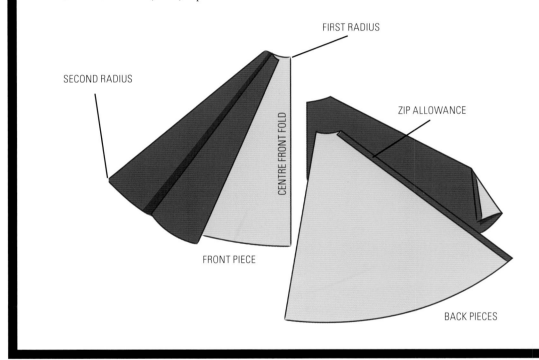

3 Cut a strip of fabric that measures 15 cm (6 in.) wide, with a length of your waist measurement plus 10 cm (4 in.). Fold the strip in half lengthways and press it. Then fold it in half widthways; this folded edge is centre front. Fold over and press a 2.5-cm (1-in.) zip-allowance strip on the open ends, folding over both layers of fabric together; this is centre back. Bring the centre front over to line up with the centre back and press. This last fold will be the side seams.

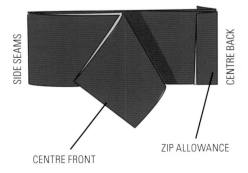

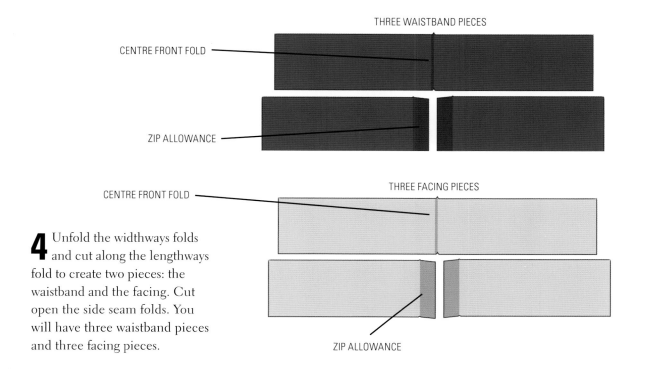

THREE WAISTBAND PIECES

CENTRE FRONT FOLD

ZIP ALLOWANCE

CENTRE FRONT FOLD

THREE FACING PIECES

4 Unfold the widthways folds and cut along the lengthways fold to create two pieces: the waistband and the facing. Cut open the side seam folds. You will have three waistband pieces and three facing pieces.

ZIP ALLOWANCE

5 Use the facing pieces as templates to cut the same shapes in fusible interfacing, but omitting the zip allowance strips at centre back. Fuse the interfacing to wrong side of the facing pieces, leaving the zip allowances as plain fabric.

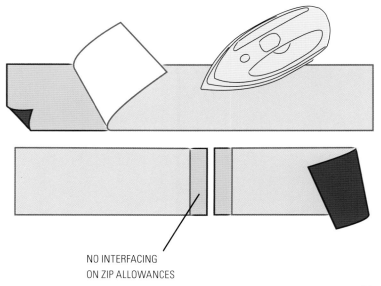

NO INTERFACING
ON ZIP ALLOWANCES

6 With right sides together and matching the centre creases, sew the front facing to the front waistband along the top edge. With right sides together, sew the back facings to the back waistbands, but stop sewing 2.5 cm (1 in.) before the zip allowance fold. Understitch the seam allowances towards the facing on all the pieces (see page 12).

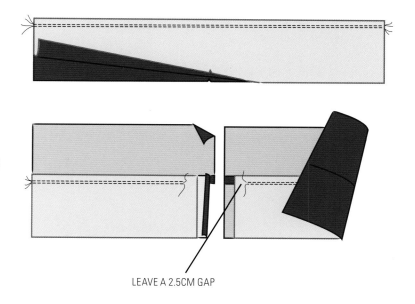

LEAVE A 2.5CM GAP

7 With right sides together and matching the centre fronts, sew the front skirt to the front waistband. With right sides together, sew the back skirt pieces to the back waistband pieces.

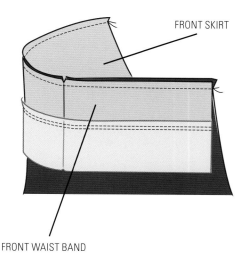

FRONT SKIRT

FRONT WAIST BAND

8 With right sides together, sew the centre backs together along the zip allowance fold, starting 18cm below the waistband and finishing at the hem.

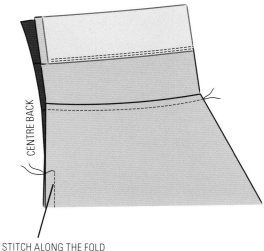

CENTRE BACK

STITCH ALONG THE FOLD

9 Insert an invisible zip (see page 15) in the skirt back, sewing it in from the top of the seam to the top of the waistband. Along the raw bottom edge of each facing, fold under and press a 1.2-cm (½-in.) hem.

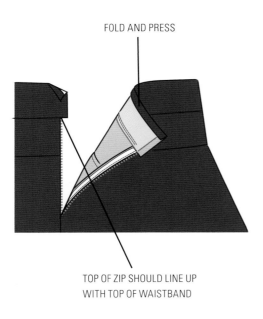

FOLD AND PRESS

TOP OF ZIP SHOULD LINE UP
WITH TOP OF WAISTBAND

10 Unfold the facing hems. With right sides together, sew the front piece to the back piece, sewing along the side seams from the raw edge of the facing right along to the hem of the skirt. Make sure the seam allowances all lie facing up towards the top of the skirt. At this stage, test the fit and make any necessary adjustments, then overlock or zigzag stitch the skirt seam allowances.

SIDE SEAM

CLIP CORNERS
OF FACING
SEAM

11 Clip the corners of the facing seam allowances as shown (also see page 12) to reduce the bulk, then press the seam allowances open.

12 Sew the open ends of the waistband and facing together along the long top edge, stopping at the zip allowance fold, then sew down the short ends. Cut off any excess zip tape and clip the corners.

CLIP CORNERS

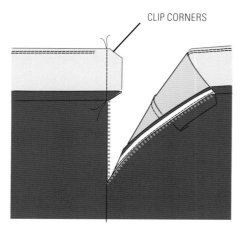

13 Fold the waistband right side out, turning out the corners neatly.

14 Turn under the hem on the facing and slipstitch it to the waistband seam allowances, just above the seam.

15 Hem the skirt using the machine-rolled technique (see page 14).

PROJECT VARIATION

The blue skirt is made from a fluid, drapey fabric. The black and white version (right) is made from a heavier printed fabric. It has also been made without a waistband, for a different look. See Double-circle Skirt, page 102, for instructions on how to construct a skirt with no waistband.

BATWING TOP

I love an easy sew, a project that only takes a couple of hours and can be jazzed up by using a fancy fabric such as velvet, can be embellished for extra wow factor, or made in a more casual fabric for lazy-day chic. I am always last minute with my outfit choices for evenings out with the girls, or sometimes I just want something new to wear to work the next morning. Whichever your preference and whatever the reason, this project is so versatile and so quick to make, and it's ideal for getting you into a cordial relationship with stretchy fabric. I recommend a two-way stretch fabric, because it is easy to handle and is more predictable, fit-wise. You will need to follow the horizontal and vertical measurement mapping system in the bodice block with the stipulated adjustments. This top can also be made as a tunic or a dress.

NOTES

Always fold fabric right sides together unless otherwise stated. It is important to press every fold to create definite creases. Take a 1.2-cm (½-in.) seam allowance throughout unless otherwise stated.

MEASUREMENTS NEEDED

HORIZONTAL MEASUREMENTS (SEE PAGE 18)
Nape to Sleeve Hem • Bust • Waist • Hip

VERTICAL MEASUREMENTS (SEE PAGE 19)
Shoulder to Waist • Shoulder to Hip

BLOCK NEEDED
Bodice Block (see page 24)

AMOUNT OF FABRIC NEEDED
This project requires a two-way stretch fabric.
Make sure the width is along the stretch of the fabric.
Width = Nape to Sleeve Hem x 4 + 5 cm (2 in.)
Length = Shoulder to Hem + 2.5 cm (1 in.)

EQUIPMENT NEEDED
Fabric • Pins • Fabric scissors
Needle and contrasting sewing thread
Tape measure • Fabric marker
Overlocker (optional) • Sewing machine
Twin needle • Sewing thread to match fabric
Iron and ironing board

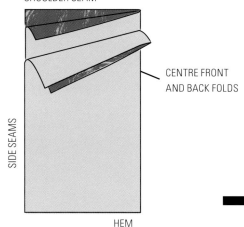

SHOULDER SEAM

CENTRE FRONT AND BACK FOLDS

SIDE SEAMS

HEM

1 Fold the fabric in half along the width and cut along the fold. Fold each piece in half along the width, press the folds, and lay one piece on top of the other, matching all edges. The top edge is the shoulder seam, the bottom edge is the hem and the folds are the centre front and back. The open edges opposite the folds are the side seams.

2 From the top corner of the centre folds, measure and mark 9 cm (3½ in.) along the shoulder seam, then measure and mark 7.5 cm (3 in.) down the centre fold. Draw a curve joining the two marks; this is the neck hole.

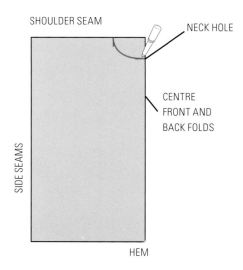

SHOULDER SEAM

NECK HOLE

CENTRE FRONT AND BACK FOLDS

SIDE SEAMS

HEM

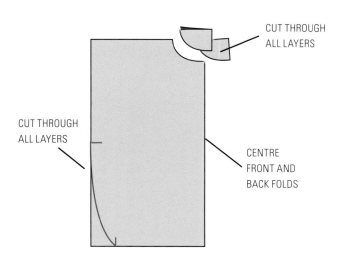

CUT THROUGH ALL LAYERS

CUT THROUGH ALL LAYERS

CENTRE FRONT AND BACK FOLDS

3 Cut along the neck hole line through all layers. From the bottom corner opposite the centre folds, measure and mark 9 cm (3½ in.) along the hem. Measure and mark the halfway point along the side seam. Join the two marks with a curved line, as shown. Cut along the line through all layers.

4 Unfold the pieces and lay one over the other, right sides together and matching all edges. Sew the shoulder seams.

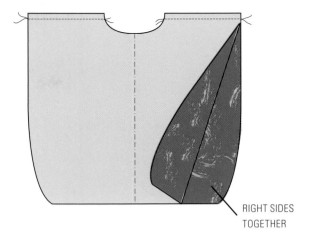

RIGHT SIDES TOGETHER

5 Open the joined pieces out flat and overlock or zig-zag stitch around the entire outer edge and around the neck hole. Turn under and sew a single hem on all the overlocked or zig-zagged edges using a twin needle attachment; this will produce two rows of stitching and is best for stretch fabrics.

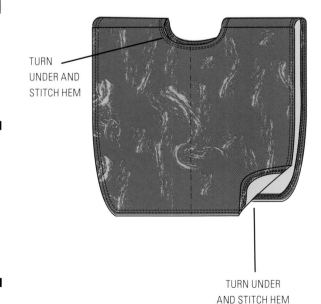

TURN UNDER AND STITCH HEM

TURN UNDER AND STITCH HEM

PROJECT VARIATION

The teal version of this top (see page 75) is made from a mediumweight jersey fabric, using a longer Nape to Sleeve Hem measurement.

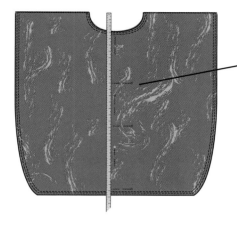

PIN THE FRONT
AND BACK PIECES
TOGETHER

6 Fold the pieces wrong sides together along the shoulder seams, matching the centre creases. Pin the layers together down the centre. Lay the tape measure along the pinned centre line, with the head level with the shoulder seams. Measure and mark 28 cm (11 in.) with a horizontal pin, then mark the rest of your vertical measurements in the same way. Visualise these marked vertical measurements as straight lines running horizontally across the fabric; the 28-cm (11-in.) mark serves as the Bust line, and the hem mark serves as the Hip line.

7 Divide all your horizontal measurements by four. Measuring out to the right from the centre line, mark with a pin the divided horizontal measurements along the corresponding vertical measurement. Join up the marks with a line of tacking in a contrasting colour, sewing through both layers.

JOIN MARKS WITH
TACKING STITCHES

8 Repeat the measuring, marking and tacking on the left-hand side of the centre line. Take out all the pins. This is a good stage at which to test the fit and make any adjustments needed. Machine sew along the lines, stopping sewing 8 cm (3 in.) above the hem. Remove the tacking stitches.

EASY CHIFFON WRAP

PROJECT VARIATION
Make the top longer (see above right) by using your Shoulder to Floor measurement (see page 19) to work out the length of the top.

Always fold fabric right sides together unless otherwise stated. It is important to press every fold to create definite creases. Take a 1.2-cm (½-in.) seam allowance throughout unless otherwise stated.

MEASUREMENTS NEEDED

Elbow to elbow; this will be the width (measure with your arms outstretched to the sides, from one elbow across your back to your other elbow) • Shoulder to desired hem length; this will be the length • Loosely measure the circumference midway between your natural waist and knee; this will be the hem circumference

AMOUNT OF FABRIC NEEDED

Width = fabric that measures 140–152 cm (55–60 in.) across from selvedge to selvedge
Length = shoulder to hem x 2 + 5 cm (2 in.)

EQUIPMENT NEEDED

Fabric • Sewing thread to match fabric
Fabric scissors • Straight ruler • Tape measure
Iron and ironing board • Fabric marker
Sewing machine

C hiffon is one of those fabrics that people fear for its ability to come alive and know its own mind. However, as unruly as this fabric may be, it can be tamed with practice. The best way to start working with a tricky fabric is with an uncomplicated project, like this top. Sometimes glorious fabrics such as a sheer chiffon in a block colour or a beautiful print, made in a simple design, can have an amazing impact. Imagine yourself on an exotic beach in your swimwear, wearing this beautiful throwover. This wonderfully flowing top is so simple to make that you don't even need to refer to the Basic Blocks section! So take your courage in both hands and go for it – a stylish, sophisticated bit of truly freehand fashion!

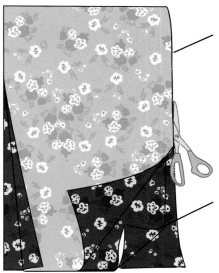

CUT ALONG THE
FOLD OF THE OUTER
LAYER ONLY

1 Fold the fabric in half along the length, then in half along the width. At the bottom edge, slip one blade of the scissors between the layers of the second fold, and cut along the outer layer right up to the corner point: the inner layer is left uncut. The cut edges are the centre front. The open edges opposite centre front are the side seams.

INNER LAYER IS UNCUT

CENTRE FRONT

2 Divide the width required by two and, with the fabric still folded, measure out from the centre front along the top edge and mark that measurement plus 2.5 cm (1 in.). Divide the hem circumference by four, measure out from the centre front along the bottom edge and mark that measurement plus 20 cm (8 in.). Join the two marks with a straight diagonal line. Cut the fabric along the drawn line, cutting through all layers.

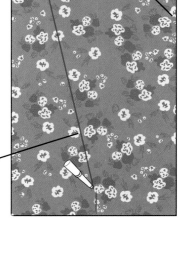

JOIN MARKS WITH
A DIAGONAL LINE

MARK ALONG
TOP EDGE

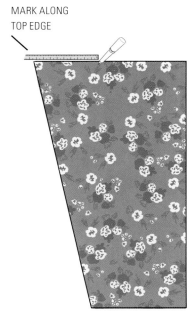

3 From the outer edge, measure and mark 24 cm (9½ in.) along the top edge. Make a little notch in the fabric at the marked point.

4 Cut along the top edge fold, cutting through all layers, from the edge to the notch; this creates the armholes.

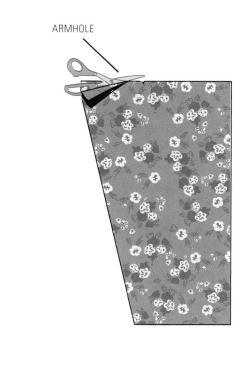

ARMHOLE

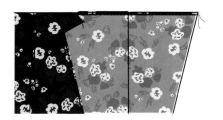

5 Unfold the fabric. Open each armhole slit out so that the edges lie in a straight line, and hem the whole armhole using a rolled hem (see page 14).

ARMHOLE   ARMHOLE

CENTRE FRONT

6 French seam (see page 10) both side seams, from the armhole edge to the hem. Hem the centre front opening and then the lower edge of the top, using a rolled hem.

FRENCH SEAMS
ON SIDE SEAMS

ROLLED HEM ON CENTRE
FRONT AND LOWER EDGE

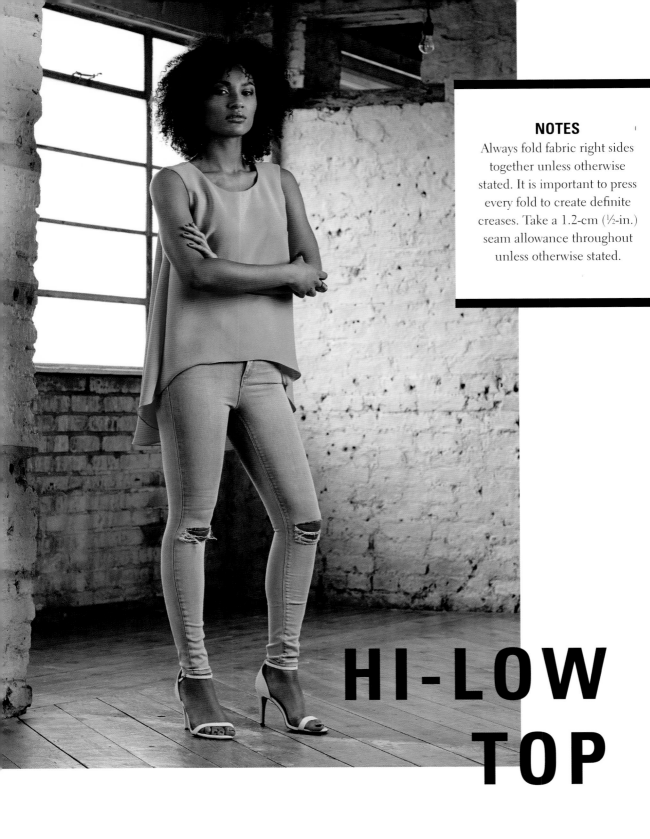

HI-LOW TOP

MEASUREMENTS NEEDED

HORIZONTAL MEASUREMENTS (SEE PAGE 18)
Back • Across Back • Across Front • Bust • Hip

VERTICAL MEASUREMENTS (SEE PAGE 19)
Shoulder to Across Back • Shoulder to Across Front
Shoulder to Bust • Shoulder to front hem
Shoulder to back hem (taken from the back)

BLOCK NEEDED
Bodice Block (see page 24)

AMOUNT OF FABRIC NEEDED
Width (along the selvedge) = shoulder to back hem
measurement x 2 + 91.5 cm (1 yd)
Length (selvedge to selvedge = at least shoulder to
back hem measurement + 25.5 cm (10 in.);
I strongly recommend getting fabric that measures
140–152 cm (55–60 in.) from selvedge to selvedge

We will be making a template for this project.
I always use poly-cotton for this, but you can
use paper if you prefer. Dimensions for the
template fabric or paper are:
Width = Hip + 30.5 cm (12 in.) ÷ 2
Length = shoulder to front hem + 11.5 cm (4½ in.)

EQUIPMENT NEEDED
Poly-cotton or paper for template • Fabric
Fusible interfacing • Tape measure • Pins • Fabric
scissors • Pinking shears • Ruler • Fabric marker
Sewing machine • Sewing thread to match fabric
Iron and ironing board

Don't you just hate it when you realise summer's here, but you still haven't quite managed to shed those Christmas kilos? Well, worry not, this über-cute top will hide all your wintry sins. This is one of those dress-up or dress-down items of clothing that are a must-have in every woman's wardrobe; depending on your choice of fabric or accessories, you can make a top to wear out on a casual lunch date with the girls or jazz it up for a night out on the town. And did I mention this can be made as a dress also? Imagine the drama of an above-the-knee or knee-length front hem in contrast with a maxi-length back hem! That's laid-back chic and a statement piece nailed in one garment.

The most suitable fabric will be anything that drapes well – for example, a viscose or a very lightweight cotton.

1 Fold the template material in half across the width and press the fold; this will be the side seam. Of the open edges opposite the fold, the top layer is the centre front and the bottom layer is the centre back. The top edge of the folded fabric is the shoulder seam and the bottom edge is the hem. With the head of the tape measure against the shoulder seam, towards the folded edge, use the fabric marker to mark the vertical measurements. Make a mark for the bust line at 16.5 cm (6½ in.); this is for the sleeveless top that we are making – if you want to have sleeves, make this mark at 20 cm (8 in.). Mark your Shoulder to Across Front measurement minus 2.5 cm (1 in.), and your Shoulder to Across Back measurement plus 2.5 cm (1 in.).

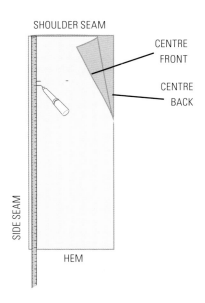

2 Visualise these marked vertical measurements as straight lines running horizontally across the fabric; each line has a corresponding horizontal measurement that is measured along it from the centre edges. Divide your Across Front measurement by two and add 1.2 cm (½ in.), and mark that measurement with a dot on the Shoulder to Across Front line. Divide your Across Back measurement by two and add 1.2 cm (½ in.), and mark that measurement with a dot on the Shoulder to Across Back line. Divide your Bust measurement by four and add 5 cm (2 in.), and mark that measurement along the Bust line with a small cross.

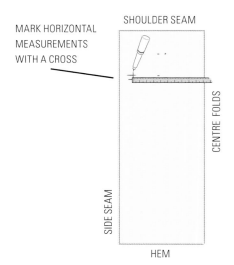

3 Divide your Hip measurement by four and add 7.5 cm (3 in.), and mark that measurement along the bottom edge with a small cross. Join the two crosses with a straight line.

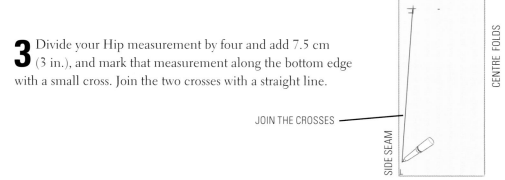

Freehand Fashion

4 From the top centre corner, measuring out along the shoulder seam, make a mark at 9 cm (3½ in.). Then divide your Back measurement by two and add 1.2 cm (½ in.) and mark that measurement on the shoulder seam. From the same corner but measuring down along the centre edges, measure and mark 5 cm (2 in.) and 10 cm (4 in.). From the 9-cm (3½-in.) mark on the shoulder seam, draw a curve down to the 10-cm (4-in.) mark on the centre edge; this is the front neck hole. From the same starting point on the shoulder seam, and following the first line for 1.2 cm (½ in.), draw a second curve down to the 5-cm (2-in.) mark; this is the back neck hole.

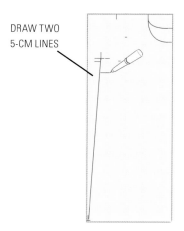

DRAW TWO
5-CM LINES

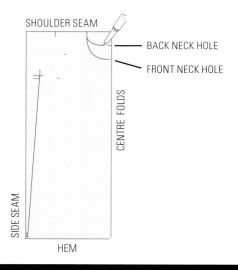

SHOULDER SEAM

BACK NECK HOLE

FRONT NECK HOLE

CENTRE FOLDS

SIDE SEAM

HEM

5 From the cross on the Bust line, draw a 5-cm (2-in.) straight line towards the centre edge. Draw another 5-cm (2-in.) line exactly 5 cm (2 in.) below the first one.

6 To create the front armhole, draw a curved line that starts at the second mark along the shoulder seam, touches the Across Front dot, and merges with the end of the 5-cm (2-in.) line drawn at Bust line level. For the back armhole, draw a second line starting at the same point as the first line and following it for 3 cm (1¼ in.), but then curving to touch the Across Back dot and merge with the end of the lower 5-cm (2-in.) line. To create the shoulder slope, measure and make a mark 2 cm (¾ in.) down the armhole line. From that mark, draw a diagonal line up to meet the edge of the neckline.

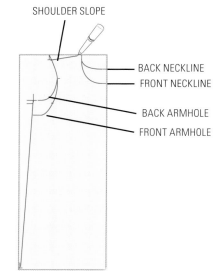

SHOULDER SLOPE

BACK NECKLINE

FRONT NECKLINE

BACK ARMHOLE

FRONT ARMHOLE

7 Measuring down from the top centre corner, mark the shoulder to front hem plus 2.5 cm (1 in.) along the centre edges. From this mark draw a curve that touches the hem 1.2 cm (½ in.) before the side seam.

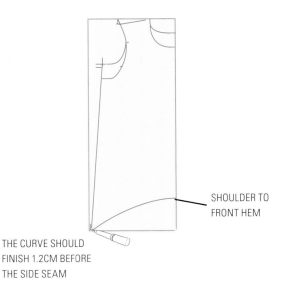

SHOULDER TO
FRONT HEM

THE CURVE SHOULD
FINISH 1.2CM BEFORE
THE SIDE SEAM

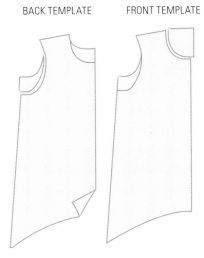

BACK TEMPLATE   FRONT TEMPLATE

8 Cut along the drawn lines through all layers, making sure to cut along only the outer markings in the armhole and neck. Transfer the remaining section of the back armhole from the front piece onto the back piece and cut it out. Then cut out the deeper front neck hole and the remaining parts of the front armhole.

9 There are only side bust darts in this garment. Working on the front template, measure 10 cm (4 in.) down the side seam from the bust line and make a mark (A). From the highest point of the shoulder seam, mark the Shoulder to Bust measurement about 10 cm (4 in.) from the centre front edge (B). Fold the fabric across these two marks and press the fold.

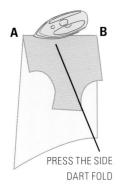

A   B

PRESS THE SIDE
DART FOLD

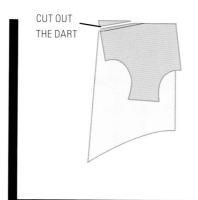

CUT OUT
THE DART

10 With the template folded along the pressed line, mark the dart. Measure down 3 cm (1¼ in.), at the side seam and draw a slanting 14-cm (5½-in.) line up to touch the fold. Cut out the dart, cutting 1 cm (⅜ in.) inside of the drawn dart line. (You will sew the dart with a 1-cm/⅜-in. seam allowance from point to edge.)

11 You can now use the templates to cut the garment pieces. Divide your Hip measurement plus 30.5 cm (12 in.) by two and measure out that length along the selvedge of the fashion fabric; cut the fabric. Fold the cut fabric in half across the length, so that the selvedges touch, and pin the front template on it, with the centre front edge lined up with the fold. Cut around the template, cutting out the dart as well.

SELVEDGES OF FASHION FABRIC

FOLD

FRONT
TEMPLATE

POSITION
TEMPLATE ON
FOLD AND PIN

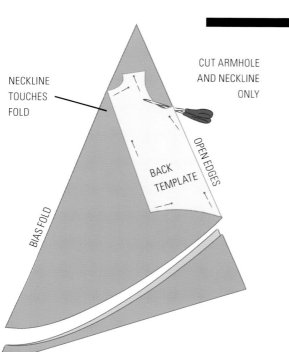

NECKLINE
TOUCHES
FOLD

CUT ARMHOLE
AND NECKLINE
ONLY

BACK
TEMPLATE

OPEN EDGES

BIAS FOLD

12 Lay the remaining piece of fabric flat and bring the cut edge over to line up with the selvedge edge. This will create a bias fold. Fit the back piece template into the pointed corner so that the side seam is lined up with the open edges and the centre of the neckline touches the fold. Pin in place.

From the highest point of the shoulder seam, measure and mark the shoulder to back hem measurement along the diagonal fold. From the side seam at the hem of the template, draw a rounded curve to touch the mark made on the fold, as shown. Cut along the drawn curve, and around the armhole, shoulder and neckline only of the template.

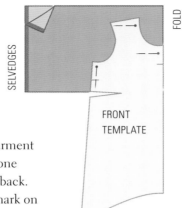

SELVEDGES

FOLD

FRONT
TEMPLATE

13 The neck and armholes of this garment have facings, which are made as one piece for the front and one piece for the back. To make the front facing, measure and mark on the front template 6.25 cm (2½ in.) from the neck hole down along the centre edge, and 6.25 cm (2½ in.) from the bustline down along the side seam. Lay the template on folded fashion fabric, with the centre front edge on the fold. Make a notch in the fashion fabric at the 6.25-cm (2½-in.) mark on the centre fold, then cut around the neck hole, shoulder seam, armhole and down to the 6.25-cm (2½-in.) on the side seam.

14 Lift the template and cut a curve as shown, linking the notch to the side seam. Make a facing for the back piece in the same way.

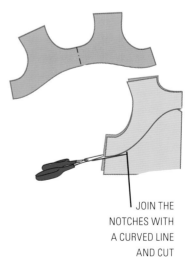

JOIN THE
NOTCHES WITH
A CURVED LINE
AND CUT

15 Use the facings as templates to cut matching pieces of fusible interfacing, then fuse the interfacing pieces to the wrong side of the facing pieces. Trim along the lower edges with pinking shears, then machine a line of straight stitch 6 mm (¼ in.) from the pinked edge.

16 Sew the side darts in the front pieces with a 1-cm (⅜-in.) seam allowance.

17 With right sides together, lay the front facing over the front piece, matching the neckline. Sew around the neckline, clip the neckline seam allowance (see page 12) and understitch the seam allowance to the facing (see page 12). Sew the armholes of the front and the facing in the same way, and clip and understitch the seam allowances.

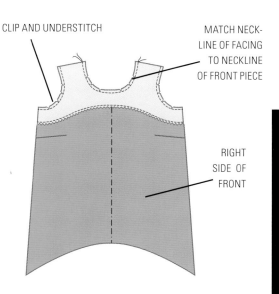

CLIP AND UNDERSTITCH

MATCH NECK-LINE OF FACING TO NECKLINE OF FRONT PIECE

RIGHT SIDE OF FRONT

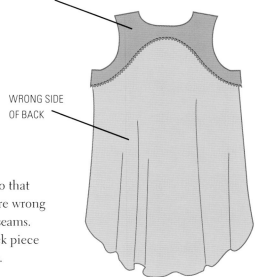

RIGHT SIDE OF FACING

WRONG SIDE OF BACK

18 Turn the facing out, so that the facing and front are wrong sides together, and press the seams. Sew the back facing to the back piece and turn out in the same way.

19 With right sides together, lay the front piece over the back piece. Lift the facings up so that they are right sides together at the side seams and carefully match the armhole facing seams on the front and back pieces. Starting from the pinked edge of the facing, sew the side seams down to the hem of the garment.

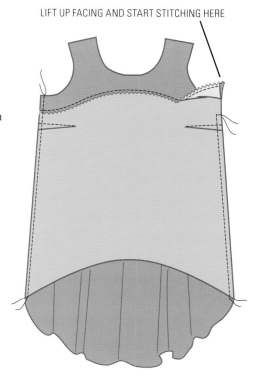

LIFT UP FACING AND START STITCHING HERE

20 Before sewing the shoulder seams, pin them and test for fit. I find that people have preferred fits when it comes to sleeveless tops: I like to have the armhole quite high up, but other people prefer it lower down. If you find that the seam allowance on the shoulders is more than 1.2 cm (½ in.), trim it down to that measurement. Tuck the shoulder of the front piece and its facing into the shoulder of the back piece and its facing. Sew the shoulder seam, then turn the top right side out.

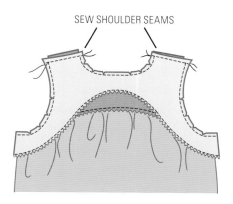

SEW SHOULDER SEAMS

21 Hem the top using a rolled hem (see page 14).

PROJECT VARIATION

I also made a hi-low dress with long sleeves. Again, use a fabric that drapes well. Follow the sleeve variation in step 1 (page 86) and create wrist-length fitted cap sleeves using the Sleeve Block (page 56). You can make your shoulder to hem and shoulder to back hem measurements as long or short as you like. Here, the front sits just above the knee and the back is maxi length.

BOX
TOP

NOTES

Always fold fabric right sides together unless otherwise stated. It is important to press every fold to create definite creases. Take a 1.2-cm (½-in.) seam allowance throughout unless otherwise stated.

MEASUREMENTS NEEDED

HORIZONTAL MEASUREMENTS (SEE PAGE 18)
Back • Across Front • Across Back • Bust
Underbust • Waist • Hip

VERTICAL MEASUREMENTS (SEE PAGE 19)
Shoulder to Across Front • Shoulder to Across Back
Shoulder to Bust • Shoulder to Underbust • Shoulder
to Waist • Shoulder to Hem • Underarm Length

OTHER MEASUREMENTS (SEE PAGE 19)
Apex • Sleeve Length
Round Sleeve

BLOCK NEEDED
Dress Block (see page 34)
Sleeve Block (see page 56)

AMOUNT OF FABRIC NEEDED

FOR THE BODICE
In fashion fabric and lining fabric
Width = Hip measurement + 35 cm (14 in.)
Length = Shoulder to Hem + 4 cm (1½ in.)

FOR THE SLEEVES
In fashion fabric and lining fabric
Width = round sleeve x 2 + 5 cm (2 in.)
Length = sleeve length + 4 cm (1½ in.)

EQUIPMENT NEEDED
Fashion fabric • Lining fabric • Invisible zip
(see page 15) • Sewing thread to match fabric
Fabric scissors • Straight ruler • Tape measure
Iron and ironing board • Fabric marker
Sewing machine • Hand-sewing needle

A box top is one of those valuable garments that hides a multitude of sins, and it has stood the test of time where trend is concerned. I love this style for its versatility; you can make it casual or very dressy, go from the office to a night out with just some accessory adjustments. It really is very easy to wear, and nails the effortless chic look. The fabric choice will determine the outcome, but if you really want to get a boxy effect, then a stiffer fabric like jacquard will not only give you boxy, but a glamorous statement piece to add to your wardrobe.

This project can be made in any length, from as short as a crop top to dress length, though you will need the dress block whichever length you choose, shortening it as needed. The sleeves can also be whatever length you want, so again, shorten them as required.

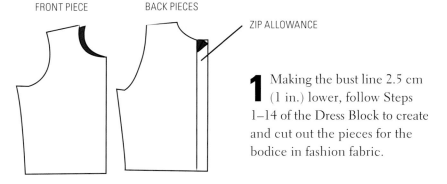

FRONT PIECE   BACK PIECES

ZIP ALLOWANCE

1 Making the bust line 2.5 cm (1 in.) lower, follow Steps 1–14 of the Dress Block to create and cut out the pieces for the bodice in fashion fabric.

2 Fold the lining fabric in half along the width. Fold over and press a 2-cm (1-in.) zip allowance strip right along the opposite edge, folding over both layers of fabric together. Lay the zip allowance fold of a back piece over this and use it as a template to cut the two lining back pieces. Press a simple fold in lining fabric, lay the centre fold of the front piece over this and use it as a template to cut the lining for the front piece.

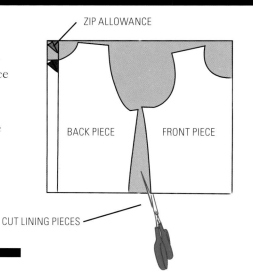

ZIP ALLOWANCE

BACK PIECE   FRONT PIECE

CUT LINING PIECES

3 Follow the darting instructions in the dress block for the side bust darts only and omit all other darts. Make the side bust darts in the fashion fabric and in the lining front pieces.

SEW BACK PIECES TOGETHER
7.5 CM DOWN FOLD

BACK PIECES

BACK LINING PIECES

4 From the neckline edge of one back piece, measure 7.5 cm (3 in.) down the zip allowance fold and make a mark. Right sides together, sew the two back pieces together along the fold line, sewing down from the neck edge to the 7.5-cm (3-in.) mark. Repeat the process with the back lining pieces.

5 Insert an invisible zip (see page 15) into the open part of the back of the fashion fabric pieces, inserting it upside down so that the zip pull will sit at the bottom edge of the fabric when the zip is closed. Right sides together, lay the joined back lining pieces over the back fashion fabric pieces. Unfold the zip allowances on all the pieces, and position the folds in the lining just behind the teeth of the zip.

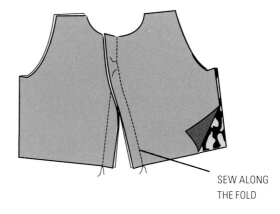

SEW ALONG
THE FOLD

6 Sew along this fold from the hem up to the point where you stopped sewing the zip. Finish sewing the seam above the zip on both lining and fashion fabrics.

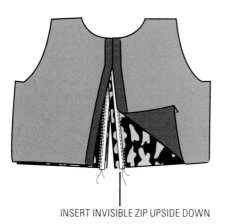

INSERT INVISIBLE ZIP UPSIDE DOWN

7 With the fashion fabric and the lining right sides together, sew the hem on either side of the zip. Clip the corner with the tip of the zip at an angle to reduce the bulk and create a neater point when turned right side out.

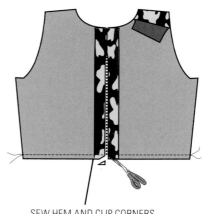

SEW HEM AND CLIP CORNERS

8 Sew the fashion fabric and lining together around the neckline, then clip the curve (see page 12). Understitch (see page 12) the seam allowances to the lining along the hem and the neckline. Then turn the back right side out, pushing out the bottom corners neatly.

SEW TOGETHER AT NECKLINE AND CLIP CORNERS

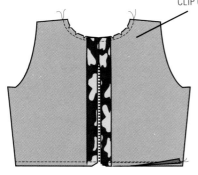

9 With right sides together, lay the front lining piece over the front fashion fabric piece. Sew around the neckline and hem, then clip the neckline curve. Understitch the seam allowances to the lining along the neckline and hem and turn the front piece right side out.

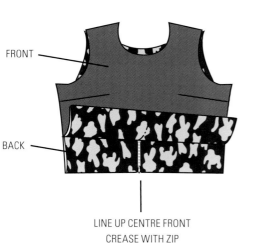

FRONT

BACK

LINE UP CENTRE FRONT CREASE WITH ZIP

10 With right sides together, lay the front piece over the back piece, aligning the centre crease of the front with the zip seam of the back. Sew the side seams of the fashion fabric pieces (but not the lining pieces).

Freehand Fashion

11 Flip the fashion fabric pieces inside so that the right sides of the lining fabric are together. Sew the side seams of the lining pieces, leaving a 12.5-cm (5-in.) gap in one of the seams for turning the top right side out once the sleeves are set in.

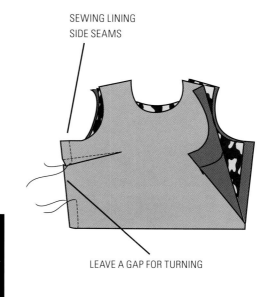

SEWING LINING
SIDE SEAMS

LEAVE A GAP FOR TURNING

12 Sew the shoulder seam from fashion fabric across to lining fabric. Clip the fashion fabric and lining joining seam to reduce bulk.

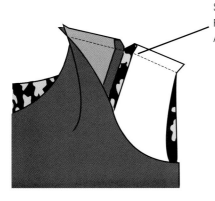

SEW ACROSS
FASHION FABRIC
AND LINING

13 Pull the fashion fabric top through the gap in the lining, so that both the fashion fabric top and the lining are wrong side out. Set aside.

14 Following the instructions for a Fitted Cap Sleeve (page 58), cut out a pair of fashion fabric sleeves and a pair of lining sleeves. Sew and set in the sleeves – lining sleeves to lining top and fashion fabric sleeves to fashion fabric top – following the instructions on pages 60–61.

FASHION FABRIC SLEEVES

LINING SLEEVES

15 Still working on the wrong side, sew the hem of the lining sleeves to the hem of the fashion fabric sleeves.

PROJECT VARIATION

The second version (right) is less boxy and more casual. The sleeves are shorter and the body is longer, and I used a pretty printed cotton fabric.

16 Turn the garment right side out through the gap in the lining and slipstitch the gap in the lining closed.

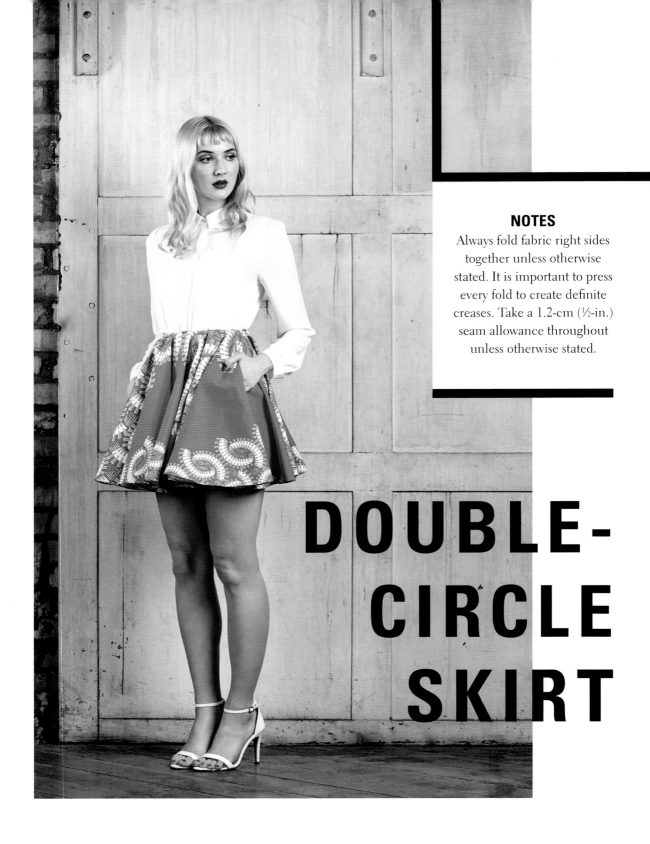

DOUBLE-CIRCLE SKIRT

MEASUREMENTS NEEDED

HORIZONTAL MEASUREMENTS (SEE PAGE 18)
Waist • Hip

VERTICAL MEASUREMENTS (SEE PAGE 19)
Waist to Hip
Skirt length (shoulder to hem minus shoulder to waist)

OTHER
1st radius = waist ÷ 3.14, ÷ 4 + 6 mm (¼ in.)
2nd radius = 1st radius + skirt length

BLOCK NEEDED

Full Flare Block (see page 48) for the outer skirt
Skirt Block (see page 42) for the lining

AMOUNT OF FABRIC NEEDED

FASHION FABRIC
Width = 2nd radius x 4 + 12.5 cm (5 in.)
Length = 2nd radius x 2 + 10 cm (4 in.)

LINING FABRIC
Width = hip measurement + 35.5 cm (14 in.)
Length = waist-to-hem measurement minus 2.5 cm (1 in.)

EQUIPMENT NEEDED
Fashion fabric • Lining fabric • Iron-on canvas
interfacing • Invisible zip (see page 15)
Sewing thread to match fabric • Fabric scissors
Tape measure • Iron and
ironing board • Fabric marker
Sewing machine • Pins

I love a full skirt with a high waist – it flatters any shape by making the waist appear smaller than it actually is. The key to success with a full skirt is getting the right kind of fullness for your body shape. If you are bottom heavy, as I am, then go for the Flare Block with this project; it is just as beautiful. This skirt is very versatile and deserves a place in every lady's bag of tricks.

Fabric choice for this skirt is entirely up to you. For a softer look, use fabric that is drapey – for example, a silk chiffon or a crepe. For a voluptuous or more structured skirt, a stiffer cotton or cottonlike fabric will work perfectly, while to amplify the drama a beautiful jacquard will offer you a scrumptious skirt to team up with a lovely top for any party.

This skirt does not feature a waistband, which I think gives it a much more modern edge.

1 Fold the fashion fabric for the outer skirt in half across the width and lay it flat, smoothing out any wrinkles. Cut along the fold.

FRONT SKIRT PIECE

ZIP ALLOWANCE

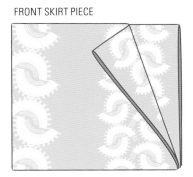

2 Fold one piece in half along the width, then fold it in half along the length; this is the front skirt piece. Fold the other piece in half across the width. Fold over and press a 2.5-cm (1-in.) zip allowance along the folded edge, folding over both layers of fabric together.

ZIP ALLOWANCE

BACK SKIRT PIECE

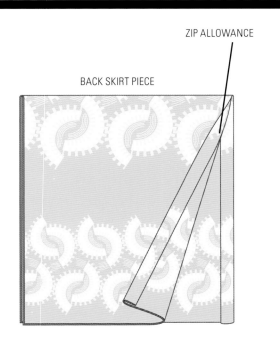

3 Then fold this piece in half along the length. This is the back skirt piece.

4 Lay the folded back piece over the folded front piece, making sure that the corners that have only folded edges on each piece are sitting over each other. If you wish, pin the layers together to stop them from slipping around while you mark and cut. Positioning the head of the tape on the point and working from the corner with only folds, pivot and use the fabric marker to mark the first radius, and then the second radius. Cut along the marked radius lines, cutting through all layers.

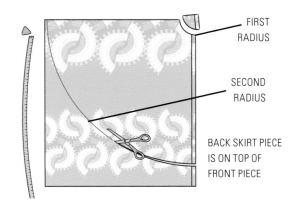

FIRST RADIUS

SECOND RADIUS

BACK SKIRT PIECE IS ON TOP OF FRONT PIECE

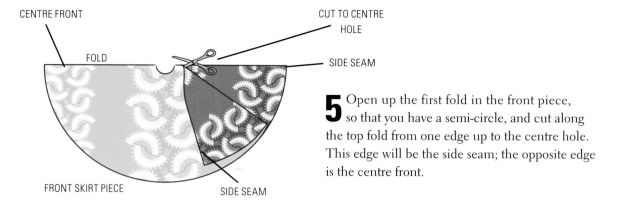

CENTRE FRONT

FOLD

CUT TO CENTRE
HOLE

SIDE SEAM

FRONT SKIRT PIECE

SIDE SEAM

5 Open up the first fold in the front piece, so that you have a semi-circle, and cut along the top fold from one edge up to the centre hole. This edge will be the side seam; the opposite edge is the centre front.

6 Open up the first fold in the back piece, so that you have a semi-circle, and cut off the folded zip allowance on one side of the centre hole; this edge will be the side seam. Cut **along** the zip allowance fold on the opposite side of the centre hole; this edge will be the centre back. You now have two pieces for the back skirt.

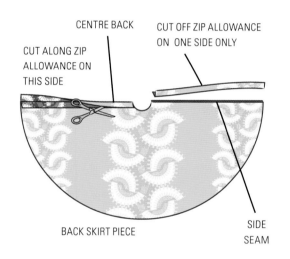

CENTRE BACK

CUT OFF ZIP ALLOWANCE
ON ONE SIDE ONLY

CUT ALONG ZIP
ALLOWANCE ON
THIS SIDE

BACK SKIRT PIECE

SIDE
SEAM

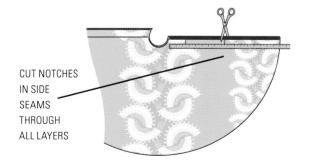

CUT NOTCHES
IN SIDE
SEAMS
THROUGH
ALL LAYERS

7 Place the two back pieces right sides together again, still as a semi-circle, and lay the folded front semi-circle on top, lining up the centre front and centre back. Measure and mark 6.5 cm (2½ in.) and 21.5 cm (8½ in.) down the side seam from the centre hole. Notch these marks with a small snip, no longer than 1 cm (⅜ in.). This is where your pockets will fit. Set the front and back pieces aside.

8 Working on the lining fabric, follow steps 1–7 of the Skirt Block on pages 44–46 – but when marking the horizontal measurement of the hem, mark it the same as the Hip measurement (this is to ensure that the lining is not too tight to walk in, but still fitted from the waist to hip, so that it holds the skirt in place). Cut out the pieces. You will have one skirt front, folded in half, and two skirt backs.

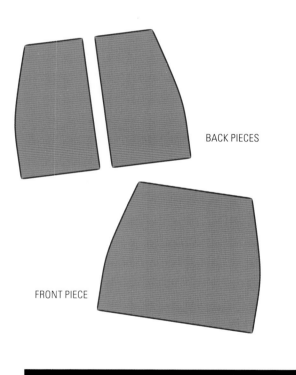

BACK PIECES

FRONT PIECE

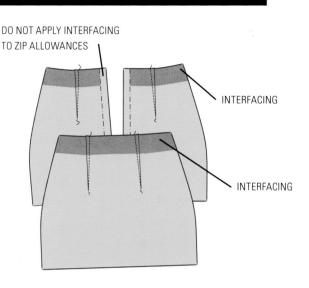

DO NOT APPLY INTERFACING TO ZIP ALLOWANCES

INTERFACING

INTERFACING

9 Cut strips of iron-on canvas interfacing 7.5 cm (3 in.) deep and the width of the lining pieces at the waist. Fuse the interfacing to the wrong side of the lining pieces, leaving the zip allowances on the back pieces as plain fabric, then trim off the excess interfacing at the side seams. Mark and sew the darts, following steps 8–11 of the Skirt Block on pages 46–47.

10 With right sides together, aligning the centre fronts and working from the centre outwards, pin the front lining and outer skirt front pieces together at the waist. (Don't worry if the outer skirt circle is bigger than the lining waist seam when it's opened out; the excess will be absorbed in the side seams.) Sew, taking a 6-mm (¼-in.) seam allowance. Snip into the seam allowance at 2.5-cm (1-in.) intervals. Understitch the seam to the lining.

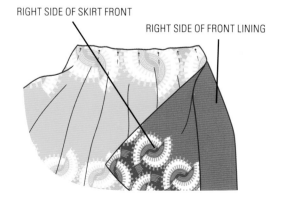

RIGHT SIDE OF SKIRT FRONT

RIGHT SIDE OF FRONT LINING

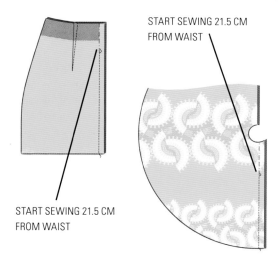

START SEWING 21.5 CM FROM WAIST

START SEWING 21.5 CM FROM WAIST

11 Pin the back skirt lining pieces right sides together along the centre back edge. Measure 21.5 cm (8½ in.) down from the waist edge along the zip allowance fold. Sew the back lining pieces together along the zip allowance fold from this point down to the hem. Repeat with the outer skirt back pieces.

12 Insert an invisible zip into the zip allowance of the outer skirt back pieces (see page 15).

13 With right sides together, lay the back lining pieces over the back outer skirt pieces, making sure that the zip allowance fold of the lining fabric lies over the zip teeth; the zip should be sandwiched between the back outer skirt pieces and the lining. Sew a seam about 3 mm (⅛ in.) behind the zip allowance fold.

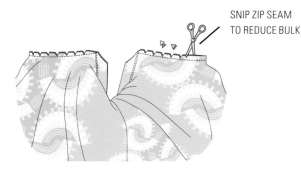

SNIP ZIP SEAM TO REDUCE BULK

14 Attach the back lining to the outer skirt at the waist, as in step 10. To reduce the bulk, snip the zip seam allowance of both the lining and outer skirt on the diagonal. Understitch the seam to the lining. Turn out.

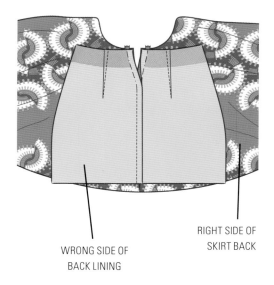

WRONG SIDE OF BACK LINING

RIGHT SIDE OF SKIRT BACK

CREATE THE IN-SEAM POCKETS

15 In-seam pockets are a really easy addition. Remember we made notches 15 cm (6 in.) apart, in the side seams of the outer skirt fabric in step 10? That will be the length of the mouth of your pocket. Use the scraps left over from the outer skirt to construct the pockets. Place four layers of fabric over each other (two sets of two layers, right sides together), with a straight edge lined up. Along the straight edge, measure and mark two 1.2-cm (½-in.) horizontal lines 15 cm (6 in.) apart. Then draw an egg shape that leans towards the marks. Before you cut out the pockets, test for fit by placing the palm of your hand inside the egg shape: there should be enough space for your palm plus a 1.2-cm (½-in.) seam allowance all around.

PLACE FOUR PIECES OF FABRIC ON TOP OF EACH OTHER

DRAW AROUND YOUR HAND TO MAKE SURE POCKET IS LARGE ENOUGH

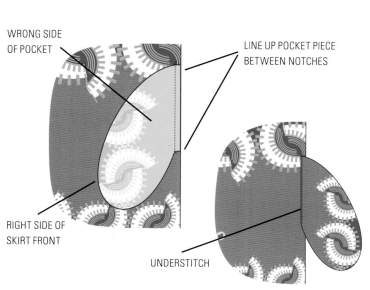

WRONG SIDE OF POCKET

LINE UP POCKET PIECE BETWEEN NOTCHES

RIGHT SIDE OF SKIRT FRONT

UNDERSTITCH

16 Separate the pockets into two pairs, still right sides together. Lay a pocket piece from one pair between the notches in one side seam of the outer front skirt, right sides together, and sew. Understitch the seam to the pockets. Attach the other pocket piece from this pair to the corresponding outer back skirt piece in the same way. then attach the other pair of pocket pieces to the other sides of the front and back pieces.

PROJECT VARIATION

You can make this skirt any length you want. For the version pictured on page 103 I made it knee length. Combined with a classic black fabric, this skirt would make a great addition to your work wardrobe.

SEW THE SIDE SEAMS

17 You are now ready to sew the side seams. Fold the outer skirt pieces up out of the way. Lay the front and back lining pieces over each other, right sides facing, making sure that the pieces are flat. Secure with pins at the waist, hip and hem level. From the centre fold, measure and mark the waist divided by 4 along the waist seam. Repeat for the hips at hip and hem levels. Join the marks with a curved line. Copy the seam allowance to the other side and sew the seams.

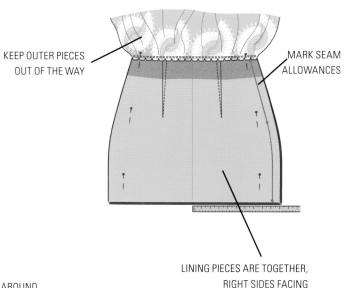

KEEP OUTER PIECES
OUT OF THE WAY

MARK SEAM
ALLOWANCES

LINING PIECES ARE TOGETHER,
RIGHT SIDES FACING

18 Place the outer skirt pieces right sides together. From the seam at the waist of the lining, sew a seam that grades to 1.2 cm (½ in.) at the pocket. Sew around the curve of the pocket and down to the hem in one continuous motion, keeping the seam allowance a consistent 1.2 cm (½ in.). Repeat on the other side.

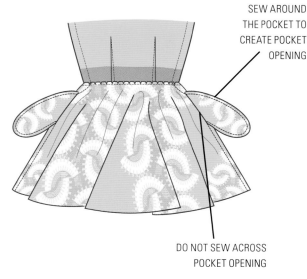

SEW AROUND
THE POCKET TO
CREATE POCKET
OPENING

DO NOT SEW ACROSS
POCKET OPENING

HEM THE SKIRT

19 Let the skirt hang for 24 hours, then hem the skirt and lining.

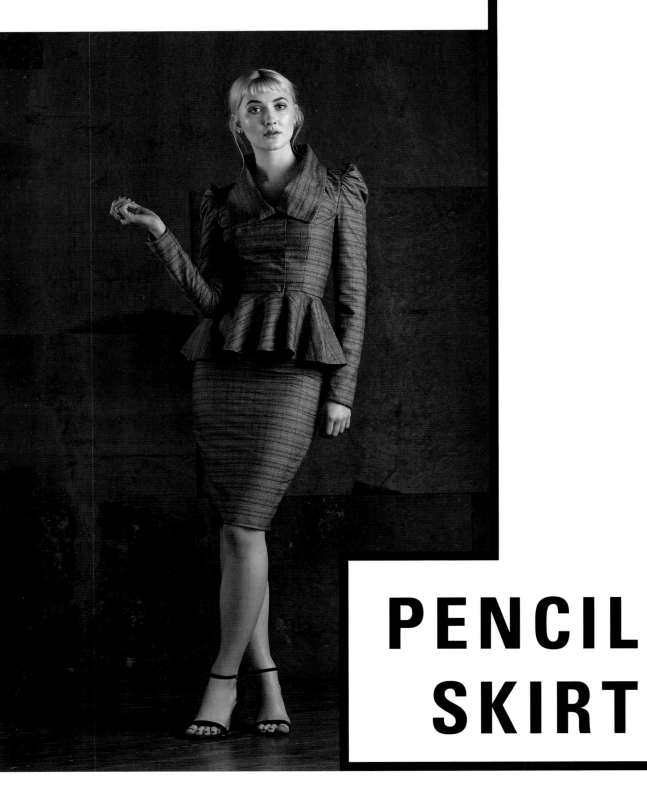

PENCIL
SKIRT

MEASUREMENTS NEEDED

HORIZONTAL MEASUREMENTS (SEE PAGE 17)
Waist • Hip

VERTICAL MEASUREMENTS (SEE PAGE 17)
Waist to Hip • Waist to hem

BLOCK NEEDED
Skirt Block (see page 42)

AMOUNT OF FABRIC NEEDED

DRESS AND LINING FABRIC
Width = Hip measurement + 35.5 cm (14 in.)
Length = waist to hem measurement + 2.5 cm (1 in.)

EQUIPMENT NEEDED
Fashion fabric • Lining fabric • Invisible zip
(see page 15) • Sewing thread to match fabric
Fabric scissors • Tape measure
Iron and ironing board
Fabric marker • Sewing machine
Pins • Hand sewing needle

NOTES
Always fold fabric right sides
together unless otherwise
stated. It is important to press
every fold to create definite
creases. Take a 1.2-cm (½-in.)
seam allowance throughout
unless otherwise stated.

A pencil skirt is so flattering and über feminine;
it gives a beautiful shape and celebrates the
female form. This skirt is a winner because it can
be made in a variety of lengths and fabrics, all of
which will give you different outcomes. The only
fabrics I avoid for pencil skirts are anything overly
drapey or soft, like chiffon. This project features a
bandless waistline, because I find this much more
flattering for most body shapes, and belt loops that
you can remove if you do not wish to wear a belt.

CUT THE PIECES

1 Following Steps 1–5 of the Skirt Block on pages 44–45, fold the fashion fabric for the outer skirt and mark out your vertical and horizontal measurements up to the point of marking out your Hip line. Along the bottom edge, which is the hem line, measure and mark your Waist divided by 4 plus 2.5 cm (1 in.) From the hem line mark, draw a straight line towards the cross at Hip level, rounding out the line as you reach the cross to imitate the natural contour of the body. Continue the curve up to the mark at the waistline. This is the side seam line.

2 Cut along the lines through all your layers. You now have two back pieces and one front piece. Use these pieces as templates to cut out the lining pieces.

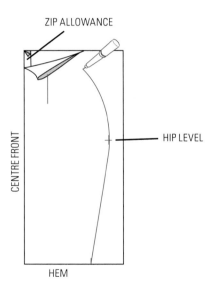

ZIP ALLOWANCE

CENTRE FRONT

HIP LEVEL

HEM

STITCH THE DARTS

3 Following Steps 8–11 of the Skirt Block on pages 46–47, mark and stitch the darts in the outer skirt and lining pieces.

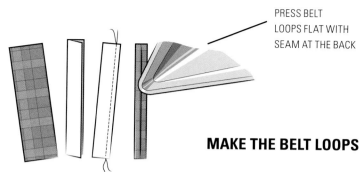

PRESS BELT
LOOPS FLAT WITH
SEAM AT THE BACK

MAKE THE BELT LOOPS

4 To create the belt loops, decide on the width of belt you would like to wear. Cut four strips of fabric that are the belt width plus 4 cm (1½ in.) by 4 cm (1½ in.). Fold the strips in half along the length and sew, taking a 1-cm (⅜-in.) seam allowance. Turn the strips right side out, fold so that the seam is in the centre, and press flat. (Placing the seam in the centre, rather than on the edge, will keep it hidden behind the belt loop.)

5 On the right side of the outer skirt pieces, from the Waist line measure the belt width plus 5 mm (¼ in.) down each dart line and pin a belt-loop strip there, seam side up. Sew across each strip, 1.2 cm (½ in.) from the edge closest to the waist. Fold the rest of the strip back up towards the waist, then sew across it 3 mm (⅛ in.) from the fold. Sew across the top of the strip to keep it in place along the waist line.

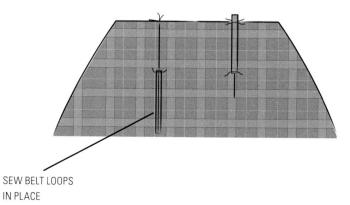

SEW BELT LOOPS
IN PLACE

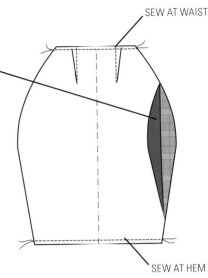

SEW AT WAIST

FRONT PIECE AND
FRONT LINING
ARE RIGHT SIDES
TOGETHER

SEW AT HEM

ASSEMBLE THE SKIRT

6 With right sides together and matching up the centre front creases, lay the front lining on the outer skirt front piece. Sew them together along the waist and hem. Understitch (see page 12) the seam to the lining at the waist and hem.

BACK LINING PIECES
ARE RIGHT SIDES
TOGETHER

7 With right sides together, lining up the zip allowance folds, place the back lining pieces on the corresponding outer skirt pieces; then place all four layers together, with the linings right sides together. Determine how high up from the hem you want your slit open, mark the spot and cut a horizontal slit across the zip allowance at that point, being careful not to cut beyond the fold.

8 With right sides together, sew the lining pieces together along the zip allowance fold, from hip level (about 23 cm/9 in. below the waist) to the top of the cut. Repeat with the outer skirt pieces.

SEW LINING
PIECES ALONG
ZIP ALLOWANCE
FOLDS

SEW OUTER BACK
PIECES ALONG ZIP
ALLOWANCE FOLDS

9 Following the instructions on page 15, insert an invisible zip into the outer skirt back piece.

PROJECT VARIATION
This version is made from a metallic print fabric. Paired with a matching Box Top (see page 94), this is power dressing at its most fashionable!

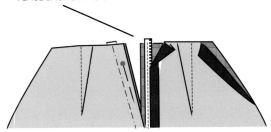

10 On the outer skirt back, undo the zip and unfold the zip allowance flaps. Lay the back lining over the top, right sides together, making sure that the zip allowance folds on each side of the lining lie on top of the teeth of the zip.

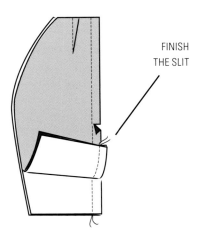

FINISH THE SLIT

11 Sew the lining and skirt pieces together just behind the teeth of the zip. Stop sewing at the same place you stopped sewing the zip. There will be a 2.5-cm (1-in.) unsewn section at the base of the zip; hand tack this section, then machine sew over the tacking, using a standard zipper foot.

12 To finish the slit, sew the left back lining and outer skirt pieces together along the zip-allowance fold from cut to hem. Repeat with the right back lining and outer skirt pieces.

HAND TACK AND THEN SEW

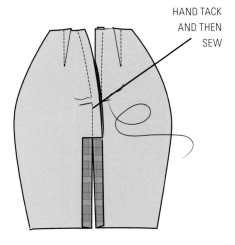

13 Sew the back lining and outer skirt together along the hem and waistline. At the top of the zip, clip the corners to reduce the bulk. Turn right side out and press. Understitch the seam to the lining.

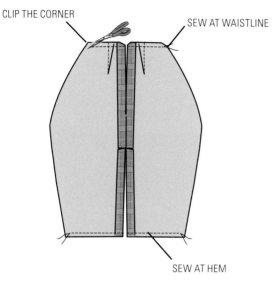

CLIP THE CORNER

SEW AT WAISTLINE

SEW AT HEM

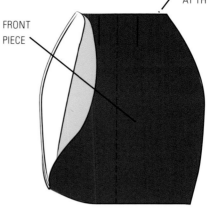

BEGIN MARKING SEAM ALLOWANCE AT THE WAIST

FRONT PIECE

14 With right sides together, lay the front piece over the back piece. Tuck the lining pieces out of the way and pin the outer skirt pieces together about 5 cm (2 in.) from the sides. From the centre, measure your Waist divided by 4 and mark with a small dash along the waist. Do the same for your Hip and hem. Join the dots with smooth curves, then copy the seam allowance to the other side seam. Sew the side seams along these lines. Do not sew the lining to the dress fabric.

15 Now turn the garment out so that the front and back linings are right sides together. Copy the seam line to the lining and sew, leaving a 15-cm (6-in.) gap in one of the lining side seams.

LEAVE A GAP IN SIDE SEAM

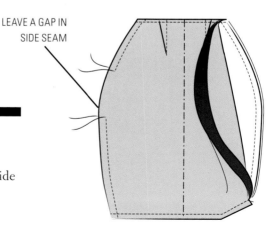

16 Turn the garment right side out through the gap and slipstitch the gap closed.

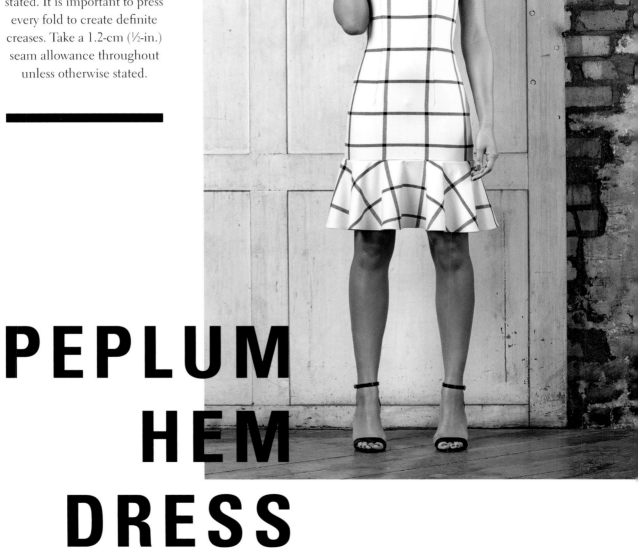

NOTES

Always fold fabric right sides together unless otherwise stated. It is important to press every fold to create definite creases. Take a 1.2-cm (½-in.) seam allowance throughout unless otherwise stated.

PEPLUM HEM DRESS

Sometimes fashion brings about a trend that will stick with you for ever! The peplum is one of those things that I don't see myself letting go of, so I just had to put it in my book for all you lovely sewists. This dress is very fashionable and I love it for its versatility; as you have probably already noticed, I like cuts that can go from work to dinner or from casual/smart daywear to nightlife. This dress is perfect for any occasion, but your fabric choice is key. Whatever fabric you decide to go with, be sure to stay away from very drapey fabrics like silk – the peplum hem needs to have some structure to get the full effect. I made my peplum hem in the same fabric as the main dress, but you could use a different fabric for contrast if you prefer; for this reason, I've listed the peplum and facing fabrics amounts separately from the dress itself (see below).

MEASUREMENTS NEEDED

HORIZONTAL MEASUREMENTS (SEE PAGE 17)
Back • Across Front • Across Back
Bust • Underbust • Waist • Hips

VERTICAL MEASUREMENTS (SEE PAGE 17)
Shoulder to Across Front • Shoulder to Across Back
Shoulder to Bust • Shoulder to Underbust
Shoulder to Waist • Shoulder to Hip
Shoulder to hem

OTHER MEASUREMENTS (SEE PAGE 18)
Apex

AMOUNT OF FABRIC NEEDED
Width = fabric that measures 140–152 cm
(55–60 in.) across from selvedge to selvedge
Length = Shoulder to hem x 2 + 5 cm (2 in.)

BLOCK NEEDED
Bodice Block (see page 24) • Dress Block
(see page 34) • Flare Block (see page 48)

AMOUNT OF FABRIC NEEDED

FABRIC FOR DRESS
Length = Shoulder to hem measurement minus
18 cm (7 in.) • Width = Hip measurement (or the
biggest horizontal measurement) + 35.5 cm (14 in.)

FABRIC FOR PEPLUM AND FACINGS
Length = 1.5–2 metres/1⅝– 2¼ yd

EQUIPMENT NEEDED
Fashion fabric • Iron-on interfacing
Zip (see page 17) • Sewing thread to
match fabric • Fabric scissors
Tape measure • Iron and ironing board
Fabric marker • Sewing machine
Overlocker (optional) • Pins

PREPARE THE BODICE

1 Following Steps 1–14 of the Bodice Block
instructions on pages 26–29, fold the fashion
fabric and mark out the vertical and horizontal
measurements, making these changes: When marking
the vertical measurements, extend the length of your
fabric to your dress length plus 2.5 cm (1 in.). When
marking the horizontal measurements, along the
hem mark your Waist measurement divided by 4
plus 7.5 cm (3 in.). Cut out all the dress pieces.

2 Following Steps 15–24 of the
Bodice Block, mark and sew
all the darts.

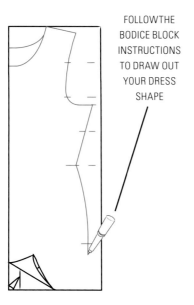

FOLLOW THE
BODICE BLOCK
INSTRUCTIONS
TO DRAW OUT
YOUR DRESS
SHAPE

CUT THE FACINGS

3 The neck and armholes of this garment have facings, which are made as one piece for the front and two pieces for the back. To make the front facing, lay the folded front dress piece on folded fashion fabric, with the centre front edge on the fold. Measure and mark 7.5 cm (3 in.) below the Bust line. Cut around the neck, shoulder and armhole, stopping at the mark you made below the Bust line.

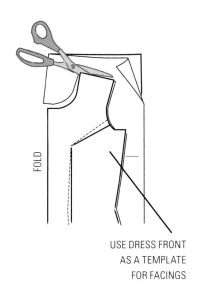

FOLD

USE DRESS FRONT
AS A TEMPLATE
FOR FACINGS

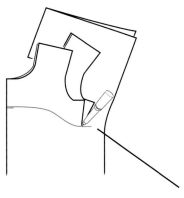

4 Lift the folded front piece off and make a mark 7.5 cm (3 in.) below the neckline centre fold of the facing. Draw a convex curve from this point to the 7.5-cm (3-in.) bust line mark you made in Step 3. Cut along the line.

JOIN THE MARKS
WITH A CURVED LINE

INTERFACE ALL
FACING PIECES

5 Use this facing as a template to cut a piece of iron-on interfacing. Fuse the interfacing to the wrong side of the front facing and overlock or zig-zag stitch the bottom edge. Make the back facings in the same way, but before you position the back piece on the facing fabric, fold over and press a 2-cm (1-in.) zip allowance strip all along the centre back edge, as in the dress. Do not apply interfacing to the zip allowances.

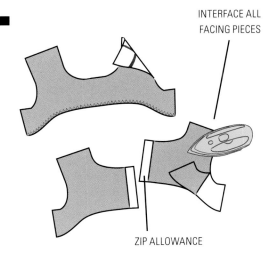

ZIP ALLOWANCE

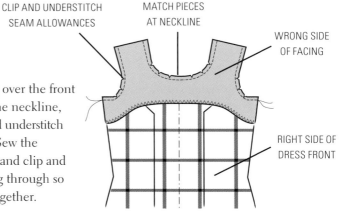

CLIP AND UNDERSTITCH SEAM ALLOWANCES

MATCH PIECES AT NECKLINE

WRONG SIDE OF FACING

RIGHT SIDE OF DRESS FRONT

ATTACH THE FACINGS

6 With right sides together, lay the front facing over the front piece, matching the neckline. Sew around the neckline, clip the neckline seam allowance (see page 12) and understitch the seam allowance to the facing (see page 12). Sew the armholes of the front and facing in the same way, and clip and understitch the seam allowances. Turn the facing through so that the facing and front piece are wrong sides together.

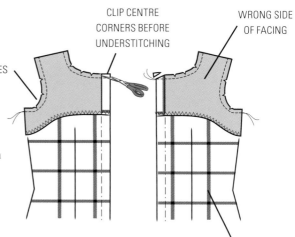

CLIP CENTRE CORNERS BEFORE UNDERSTITCHING

WRONG SIDE OF FACING

CLIP AND UNDERSTITCH SEAM ALLOWANCES

7 Sew the back facings to the back pieces in the same way, continuing the stitching over the zip allowance fold. When you clip the neckline, also clip the centre corners to reduce the bulk, before understitching the seam to the facing. Turn the facings through so that the facings and back pieces are wrong sides together.

RIGHT SIDE OF DRESS BACK

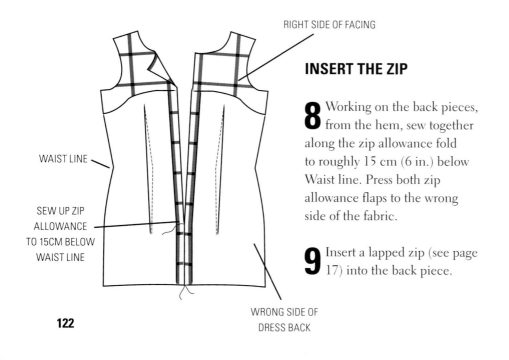

RIGHT SIDE OF FACING

WAIST LINE

SEW UP ZIP ALLOWANCE TO 15CM BELOW WAIST LINE

INSERT THE ZIP

8 Working on the back pieces, from the hem, sew together along the zip allowance fold to roughly 15 cm (6 in.) below Waist line. Press both zip allowance flaps to the wrong side of the fabric.

9 Insert a lapped zip (see page 17) into the back piece.

WRONG SIDE OF DRESS BACK

ASSEMBLE THE DRESS

10 With right sides together, lay the front dress over the back dress, lining up the centre front over the zip. Following Steps 23–26 of the Dress Block on page 41, mark your Bust, Underbust, Waist, and Hip measurements, each divided by four, along the relevant horizontal levels. Join the marks, as in Step 6 of the Dress Block; this line is the seam line. To mark the hem, measuring from the centre fold, measure the waist divided by 4 plus 5 cm (2 in.) Pull the side seams of the facings up, so that they're right sides together.

LINE UP CENTRE FRONT AND ZIP

PULL FACINGS UP SO THEY ARE RIGHT SIDES TOGETHER

MARK BUST, UNDERBUST, WAIST AND HIPS

RIGHT SIDES TOGETHER

START STITCHING HERE

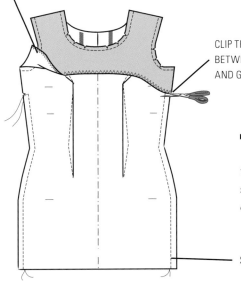

CLIP THE SIDE SEAM BETWEEN FACINGS AND GARMENT PIECES

11 Starting from the overlocked or zig-zagged edge of the facing, sew the side seams down to the bottom edge of the dress, then test the fit. Once you are happy, clip the side seam between the facings and the main garment pieces, then overlock or zig-zag the seam.

SEW BOTH SIDES SEAMS

RIGHT SIDE OF BACK

WRONG SIDE OF FACING

12 Turn the back facing inside out. Tuck the shoulder of the front piece and its facing into the shoulder of the back piece and its facing. Sew across the shoulder seam and snip the corners, then turn the back facing right side out.

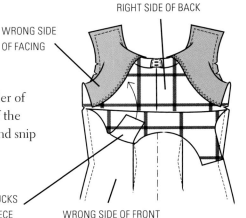

SHOULDER OF FRONT PIECE TUCKS INSIDE SHOULDER OF BACK PIECE

WRONG SIDE OF FRONT

ATTACH THE PEPLUM HEM

13 Measure the circumference of the dress hem. Divide this by 3.14 and then divide the answer by 2. This will give you a decimal number; round this number DOWN to the nearest whole or .5 number. This is your first radius; your second radius is your first radius plus 23 cm (9 in.). Using these radii, follow Steps 1–3 of the Full Flare Block instructions on pages 52–53 to cut out the fabric for the peplum hem.

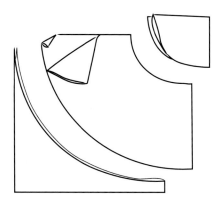

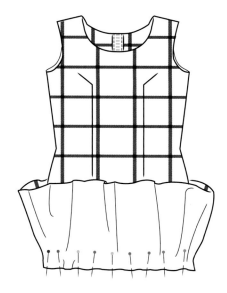

14 With right sides together, pin then stitch the inner edge of the circle to the hem of the skirt. Overlock or zig-zag the seam.

HEM THE DRESS

15 Hang the dress for 24 hours, then turn under and stitch a narrow double hem or overlock and turn and stitch a single hem.

DATE NIGHT DRESS

When better to make an impact than on a first date or a night out with that someone special? This classic lace dress is simple, clean, elegant and sexy, without being too in your face, and I love it for all those reasons. I recommend using guipure lace to achieve this look perfectly. Choose one that features a pattern that is not blatantly repetitive, as this will give you a better neckline and you won't have to worry about matching the pattern.

NOTES

Always fold fabric right sides together unless otherwise stated. It is important to press every fold to create definite creases – but test the iron temperature on a scrap piece of lace first! Take a 1.2-cm (½-in.) seam allowance throughout unless otherwise stated. Be sure to leave the decorative edge on one selvedge of the lace, so that you can use it as the hem. I have used an acetate lining for my first lining, and poly-cotton for the second lining. I like the slight sheen of the acetate behind the lace – I just don't like it against my skin. I chose poly-cotton for the second lining because it is strong and acts like control wear, smoothing out the curves under the dress, and it is breathable.

MEASUREMENTS NEEDED

HORIZONTAL MEASUREMENTS (SEE PAGE 18)
Back • Across Front • Across Back • Bust • Underbust
Waist • Hip • Round Sleeve • Round Elbow • Wrist

VERTICAL MEASUREMENTS (SEE PAGE 19)
Shoulder to Across Front • Shoulder to Across Back
Shoulder to Bust • Shoulder to Underbust
Shoulder to Waist • Shoulder to Hip • Shoulder to hem
Sleeve Length • Underarm Length • Elbow Length

OTHER MEASUREMENTS (SEE PAGE 19)
Apex • Hollow to Dip

BLOCK NEEDED
Dress Block (see page 34) • Sleeve Block (see page 56)

AMOUNT OF FABRIC NEEDED

LACE FOR THE DRESS
Width = largest horizontal measurement + 35.5 cm (14 in.)
Length = shoulder to hem measurement + 2.5 cm (1 in.)

LACE FOR THE SLEEVES
Width = Round Sleeve x 2 + 5 cm (2 in.)
Length = Sleeve Length plus 4 cm (1½ in.)
Note: Add an additional 13 cm (5 in.) to the sleeve length for a pleated or puffed sleeve (see pages 60–63).

FIRST LINING AND SECOND LINING
Width = largest horizontal measurement + 35.5 cm (14 in.)
Length = shoulder to hem

EQUIPMENT NEEDED
Guipure lace • Acetate lining fabric for first lining
Poly-cotton for second lining • Invisible zip (see page 15)
Sewing thread to match fabric, plus contrasting thread for tacking • Fabric scissors • Tape measure
Iron and ironing board • Fabric marker
Sewing machine • Hand sewing needle • Pins
Invisible zipper foot (optional)

CUT THE PIECES

1 Working on the first lining, fold the fabric following Steps 1–2 of the Dress Block (page 36). Before mapping your measurements, measure the shoulder to hem from the hem upwards; this is so that you can use the lace edge detail for the hem. Mark your measurements, following Steps 3–12 of the Dress Block. Cut out the pieces, but do not cut a neckhole yet just; instead, snip a 1.2-cm (½-in.) notch at the point where the inner shoulder seam will meet the neckline.

2 Fold the lace in half across the width and lay it flat, smoothing out any wrinkles: this fold is the centre front. Fold over a 2.5-cm (1-in.) zip allowance strip right along the opposite edge, folding over both layers of fabric together. This folded edge is the centre back. The top edge is the shoulder seam and the bottom edge is the hem.

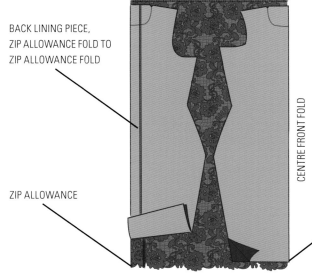

BACK LINING PIECE, ZIP ALLOWANCE FOLD TO ZIP ALLOWANCE FOLD

ZIP ALLOWANCE

CENTRE FRONT FOLD

3 Lay the front first lining piece over the lace, fold to fold, with the hem 2.5 cm (1 in.) above the lace edge. Do the same with the back lining piece, zip allowance fold to zip allowance fold. Use the lining pieces as templates to cut out the lace pieces.

FRONT LINING PIECE SHOULD SIT 2.5CM ABOVE THE LACE EDGE

4 Unfold the back and front pieces of the lace fabric and cut your neckline, following the natural detail in the lace. Try to do this as evenly as possible – but bear in mind that, depending on the pattern of your lace, your neckline may not be symmetrical; what you are looking for is a good balance.

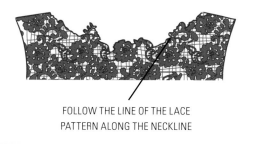

FOLLOW THE LINE OF THE LACE
PATTERN ALONG THE NECKLINE

MEASURE 10CM
DOWN FROM
SHOULDER SEAM

SHOULDER SEAM

FOLD

HOLLOW TO DIP

5 Now create a sweetheart neckline on the front lining. With the front lining still folded along the centre front line, measure 10 cm (4 in.) down from the shoulder seam along the armhole and make a mark. From the top edge of the centre fold, measure and mark your Hollow to Dip (see page 18) minus 1.2 cm (½ in.). From the mark in the armhole, draw a convex curve that reaches the mark on the fold. Cut along the line.

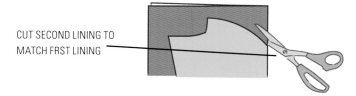

CUT SECOND LINING TO
MATCH FIRST LINING

6 Fold the second lining fabric, following Steps 1–2 of the Dress Block (page 36). Lay the first lining piece that you cut in Step 5 on top, fold to fold, and use it as a template to cut the second lining front piece.

7 For the back lining, mark 12.5 cm (5 in.) down the armhole level and draw a line straight across to the centre back, crossing over the zip allowance fold. Cut along the line. Use this to cut an identical second lining piece for the back.

CUT SECOND LINING TO
MATCH FIRST LINING

CUT 10CM OFF THE TOP
OF THE BACK LINING PIECE

CREATE THE DARTS

8 Lay the first and second front lining pieces over the front lace piece; all the pieces should be folded. Following Steps 15, 17 and 18 of the Dress Block, make the vertical and side bust dart creases through all the layers. Do NOT invert the wrong facing dart folds yet.

9 Still working on the front pieces, unfold the lace and the first lining. Lay the first lining against the lace, with the right side of the lining facing the wrong side of the lace. Tack along the dart creases, through the lining and lace, to hold the pieces together. Then invert the dart folds so that all are projecting on the wrong side of the lining.

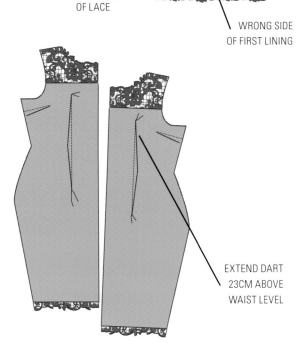

WRONG SIDE
OF LACE

WRONG SIDE
OF FIRST LINING

10 Mark the darts in the lined lace piece and the second lining, following Steps 20–21 of the Dress Block.

11 Repeat Steps 8–10 for the back pieces, following the back dart instructions in the Dress Block but extending the dart to 23 cm (9 in.) above the waist level. Sew all the darts.

EXTEND DART
23CM ABOVE
WAIST LEVEL

ASSEMBLE THE DRESS

12 Hem the first lining on both the front and back pieces using a machine–rolled hem (see page 14).

13 Lay the front of the dress on your work surface, right (lace) side up. Along the neckline, pull down the lace so that the right side of the attached lining is exposed, then lay the second lining over this, right sides together. Sew along the sweetheart neckline only, then clip the neckline and understitch the seam to the second lining.

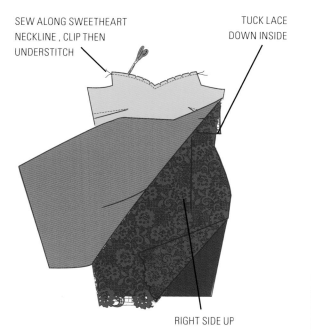

SEW ALONG SWEETHEART NECKLINE , CLIP THEN UNDERSTITCH

TUCK LACE DOWN INSIDE

RIGHT SIDE UP

14 Repeat steps 13 and 14 with the back pieces along the lining neckline, but stop sewing about 2.5 cm (1 in.) before you reach the zip allowance fold.

15 Pin the second lining out of the way of the zip allowance fold, then tack the first lining to the lace along the zip allowance fold.

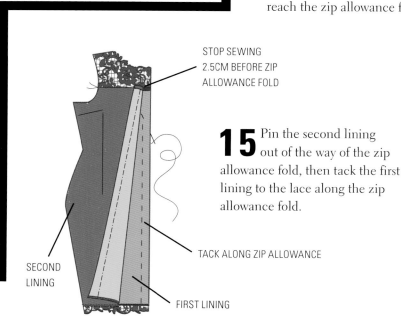

STOP SEWING 2.5CM BEFORE ZIP ALLOWANCE FOLD

TACK ALONG ZIP ALLOWANCE

SECOND LINING

FIRST LINING

16 Insert an invisible zip in the lace and first lining, following the instructions on page 15. With the back folded in half, right sides together, make a horizontal snip in the lace zip allowance to the fold, at the level of the lining.

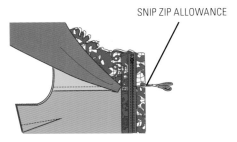

SNIP ZIP ALLOWANCE

17 Bring the second lining over to lie on the lace, right sides together. The shoulder section of the lace will be sandwiched between the second and first linings. Note that the seam allowance should be folded outwards on both linings, at the top of the seam. Sew along the zip allowance fold up to the end of the zip and turn out.

18 Sew the centre back of the second lining along the zip allowance fold.

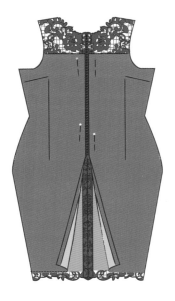

19 Place the front dress on the back dress, right sides together, and ensure that it is flat, except for the bust. Pull the front second lining piece out of the way and pin the sides of the dress at the Bust, Waist and Hip levels.

Freehand Fashion

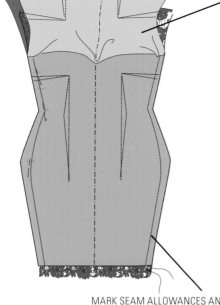

PULL THE SECOND LINING
OUT OF THE WAY

20 Measuring from the centre, mark the Bust divided by 4 along the bust line. Repeat for the Underbust, Waist and Hip. At the hem just measure 2.5 cm (1 in.) inside the side seam and mark. Join the marks and copy the seam allowance to all your side seams. Sew along the lines.

MARK SEAM ALLOWANCES AND
THEN SEW BOTH SIDE SEAMS

21 Sew the shoulder seams, then tack the two linings to the bottom half of the armhole.

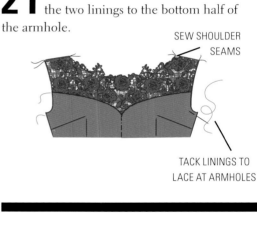

SEW SHOULDER
SEAMS

TACK LININGS TO
LACE AT ARMHOLES

22 Cut the sleeves from lace fabric only, following Steps 1–7 of the Sleeve Block (page 58–59). Set in the sleeves, following the instructions for a standard fitted sleeve head on page 60.

23 Hem the second lining using a machine–rolled hem (see page 14).

VELVET WRAP DRESS

NOTES

Always fold fabric right sides together unless otherwise stated. It is important to press every fold to create definite creases. Take a 1.2-cm (½-in.) seam allowance throughout unless otherwise stated. With all notches in this project, cut small straight snips rather than cutting out wedge shaped chunks.

MEASUREMENTS NEEDED FOR THE DRESS

HORIZONTAL MEASUREMENTS (SEE PAGE 18)
Back • Across Front • Across Back • Bust
Underbust • Waist • Hip • Round Sleeve
Round Elbow • Wrist

VERTICAL MEASUREMENTS (SEE PAGE 19)
Shoulder to Across Front • Shoulder to Across Back
Shoulder to Bust • Shoulder to Underbust
Shoulder to Waist • Shoulder to Hip
Shoulder to Hem • Sleeve Length
Underarm Length • Elbow Length

OTHER MEASUREMENTS (SEE PAGE 19)
Apex • Waist difference (the difference between
your shoulder to waist and your back length)

BLOCKS NEEDED
Dress Block (see page 34)
Sleeve Block (see page 56)

AMOUNT OF FABRIC NEEDED

SKIRT FABRIC
Width = Hip measurement + 25 cm (10 in.)
Length = shoulder to hem measurement minus
Shoulder to Waist measurement + 23 cm (9 in.)

BODICE FABRIC
Width = largest horizontal measurement between
the Bust and Waist + 38 cm (15 in.)
Length = Shoulder to Waist measurement
+ 2.5 cm (1 in.)

SLEEVE FABRIC
Width = Round Sleeve x 2 + 5 cm (2 in.)
Length = Sleeve Length + 4 cm (1½ in.)

MATERIALS AND EQUIPMENT NEEDED
Medium-weight stretch fabric • Soft iron-on
interfacing • Sewing thread to match fabric
Fabric scissors • Straight ruler • Tape measure
Iron and ironing board • Fabric marker • Sewing
machine • Overlocker (optional) • Twin needle
(optional) • Hand sewing needle • Pins

Those of you who saw the second series of the
Great British Sewing Bee may remember this
little number, which won me the Garment of the
Week prize in week four of the competition. It's a
combination of my favourite things about sewing
women's fashion: its style and cut celebrate the
female form as it wraps around and hugs the body,
flattering every contour, while the velvet fabric
suggests luxury and glamour and is my ultimate
favourite fabric. My garment of the week included
small shoulder pads and some embellishment to
one shoulder, but I have left this one plain so you
can see just how beautiful it is, even without the
added ding-dongs.

This style requires stretchy fabric, and I
recommend that you use a medium to medium-
heavy weight. If the fabric is too light, you will lose
the strength of the draping, whereas if it's too heavy,
it will be far too bulky and lose its elegance. Stretch
velvet, also known as velour, is the perfect weight
for this, despite my obvious bias. Feel free to play
around with the style; make it a different length
(I've made it ankle length in the past and it looked
amazing), make the sleeves a different length, add
embellishment or try a completely different stretch
fabric. The possibilities are vast, so make this one
your own!

CUTTING THE SKIRT

1 Working on the skirt fabric, fold the fabric in half across the width. The fold is the centre back, the top edge is the waist edge, the open edge opposite the fold is the front and the bottom edge is the hem. From the centre back, measure and mark your Waist divided by 2. From that first mark, measure and mark 9 cm (3½ in.) in towards the centre back.

3 Working on the waist again, measuring from the centre back, mark your Waist divided by 4. Measuring down from the Waist, mark your Waist difference divided by 2 along the centre back. Draw a curve from here to the quarter waist point.

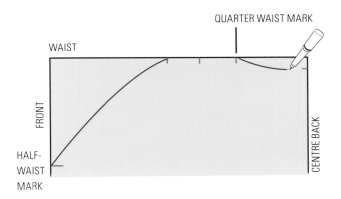

2 From the waist, measure and mark 18 cm (7 in.) down the front. Draw a curve from the half waist mark down to the 18-cm (7-in.) mark on the front. Working along the hem, measure and mark 11.5 cm (4½ in.) from the centre back. Draw a curve that connects this mark to the 18-cm (7-in.) mark on the front.

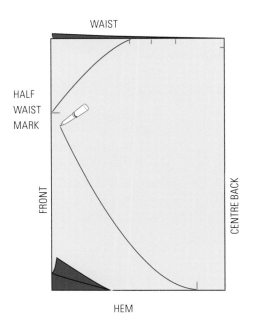

4 Cut along your lines, then cut a tiny straight snip at the centre back and at the second and third marks along the waist. Set the skirt aside.

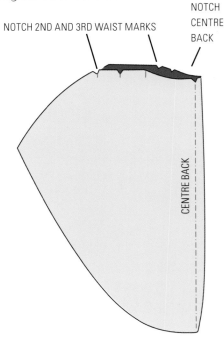

CUTTING THE BODICE

5 Now work on the bodice; we will cut the back piece first and then use it as a template to cut part of the front piece. Fold your bodice fabric in half across the width. This fold is the centre back, and the bottom edge is the Waist line. Following Steps 3–12 of the Dress Block instructions on page 34, mark out the vertical and horizontal measurements, making these changes: when marking your horizontal measurements, omit the 5 cm (2 in.) usually added after dividing the measurement by 4. Mark the neck hole 4 cm (1½ in.) down the centre back edge, as you need the back neckline to be higher for this style. Omit the 5-cm (2-in.) straight line at the Bust line. Remember this is the back piece, so when marking the armhole, ignore the Shoulder to Across Front and the Across Front markings.

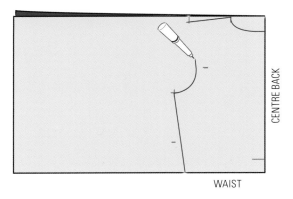

CENTRE BACK

WAIST

6 Along the centre back, measure up from the waist and mark your waist difference divided by 2. Draw a curved line from this point to the side seam at waist level. Cut out the back piece.

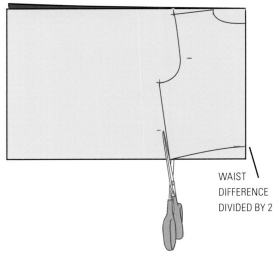

WAIST DIFFERENCE DIVIDED BY 2

7 From the opposite end of your bodice fabric, draw a straight line parallel to the edge 18 cm (7 in.) in from the edge; this is your centre front line. Along the bottom edge, draw a straight line across 6 cm (2½ in.) up from the edge.

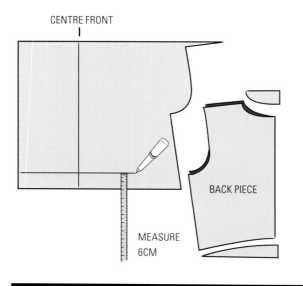

CENTRE FRONT

MEASURE 6CM

BACK PIECE

9 Remove the back piece. Mark your Shoulder to Across Front measurement on the vertical line that you drew in step 7. Then divide your Across Front measurement by two, add 1.2 cm (½ in.) and mark with a small cross on the Shoulder to Across Front line. Cut along the straight line at the bottom. Mark the front armhole and cut it out.

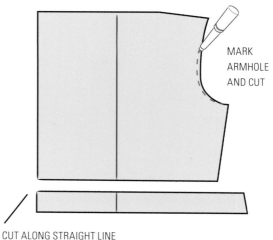

MARK ARMHOLE AND CUT

CUT ALONG STRAIGHT LINE

8 Lay the centre back fold of the back piece along the centre front line. Cut around the side seams from the 6-cm (2½-in.) line up, and along the shoulder seam.

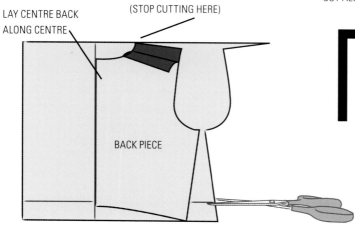

CUT TO SHOULDER SEAM (STOP CUTTING HERE)

LAY CENTRE BACK ALONG CENTRE

BACK PIECE

START CUTTING AT 6 CM MARK

10 Measure the length from the highest point of the shoulder straight down to the base. From this same point, which should be 9 cm (3½ in.) from the centre front line, pivot and mark the same length at regular intervals extending to the edge of the fabric. Along the base, measure and mark 9 cm (3½ in.) from the centre front line, towards the side seam.

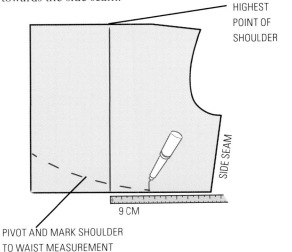

HIGHEST POINT OF SHOULDER

SIDE SEAM

9 CM

PIVOT AND MARK SHOULDER
TO WAIST MEASUREMENT

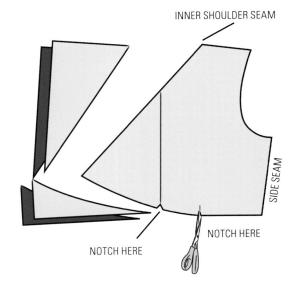

INNER SHOULDER SEAM

SIDE SEAM

NOTCH HERE

NOTCH HERE

NOTCH HERE

11 From the inner shoulder seam (9 cm/3½ in. from the centre front line) draw a straight line that connects to the end of the curved line drawn in step 10. Cut along this line and the curved base. Notch the bottom of the centre front line and the mark 9 cm (3½ in.) from the centre front line along the base.

12 For the waistband, cut a strip of fabric that measures your Waist measurement divided by two by 7.5 cm/3 in. The waistband needs to be stabilized because of the gathers that will be pulling on both ends of it. Cut a piece of iron-on interfacing the same size and fuse it to the wrong side of the waistband. Notch the centre of the waistband along both long edges.

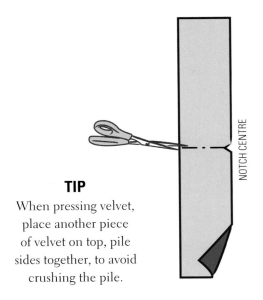

NOTCH CENTRE

TIP

When pressing velvet, place another piece of velvet on top, pile sides together, to avoid crushing the pile.

13 Following the instructions in the Sleeve Block (page 56), cut two Fitted Cap sleeves.

ASSEMBLING THE DRESS

14 Right sides together, place the front bodice pieces on the back bodice piece, aligning the shoulders, then sew or overlock the shoulder seams.

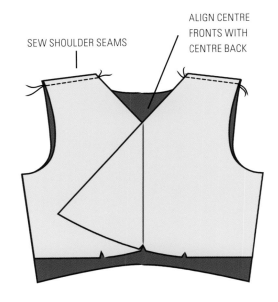

SEW SHOULDER SEAMS

ALIGN CENTRE FRONTS WITH CENTRE BACK

15 Overlock or zig-zag the entire neckline, and the hem and front of the V-section of the skirt. Turn under a single hem along the overlocked or zig-zagged edges. You can either sew this down with a twin needle attachment or blind hem it by hand.

16 With your machine set to the longest stitch length – this is 5 for most models – sew two rows of straight stitches 6 mm (¼in.) apart, between the edge and the first notch on both ends of the waist seam for the skirt, and between the edge and the first notch on the front bodice pieces. These are gathering stitches. Gather these sections so that they fit the space between the two notches.

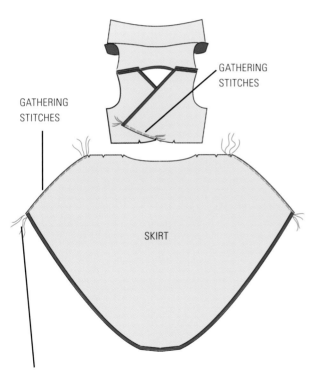

GATHERING STITCHES

GATHERING STITCHES

SKIRT

PULL ON ENDS TO GATHER THE STITCHES

17 Working on the front bodice, lay the centre notches over one another so that the right front is on top of the left front. The gathered sections should fit into the spaces between the centre notches and the other notch along the edges as the front pieces cross over. Matching the centre notches, lay the waistband over this, right sides together. Pin in place and sew or overlock in place.

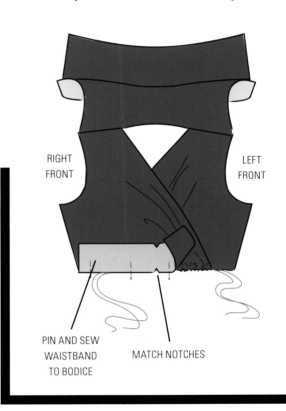

RIGHT FRONT

LEFT FRONT

PIN AND SEW WAISTBAND TO BODICE

MATCH NOTCHES

18 With right sides together, sew or overlock the side seams of the bodice, taking a 1-cm (⅜-in.) seam allowance.

20 Then wrap the skirt front pieces over each other, matching up the centre notches with the centre notch on the waistband and making sure that the right end is wrapped before the left end. Pin in place.

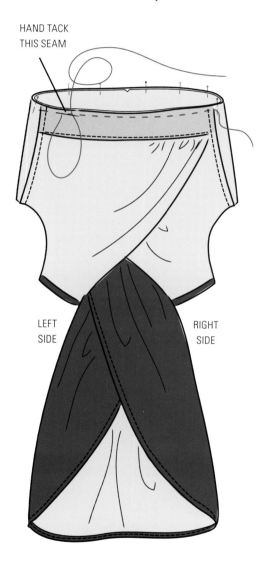

HAND TACK
THIS SEAM

LEFT
SIDE

RIGHT
SIDE

19 Match the centre back notches of the bodice and skirt together, right sides together, and pin in place.

21 Pin the rest of the skirt to the waist seam of the bodice, stretching it to fit if need be. Sew or overlock this seam, taking a 1-cm (⅜-in.) seam allowance. I strongly recommend that you hand tack this seam first.

22 Sew or overlock the side seam of the sleeves, then zig-zag or overlock the hem of the sleeve. Turn a single fold hem, then sew this down with a double needle or blind stitch by hand.

23 Sewing the sleeve to the bodice is much easier with stretch fabric; simply match up the side seams of the sleeve and bodice, right sides facing, then match up the notch at the centre of the sleeve head with the shoulder seam. Pin these points in place, then stretch the armhole and sleeve together as you sew or overlock the sleeve to the bodice.

Freehand Fashion

WRAP-AROUND MAXI DRESS

NOTES

Always fold fabric right sides together unless otherwise stated. It is important to press every fold to create definite creases. Take a 1.2-cm (½-in.) seam allowance throughout unless otherwise stated.

This wrap dress is perfect from spring right through the summer and into autumn. I love any garment that fits and flatters and that's exactly what this dress will do for most body shapes. The fitted waistband, plunging neckline and full but light skirt are a guaranteed celebration of your body. This moderately easy project offers a dress that deserves to follow you on holiday. It is quite straightforward – no lining and no zip – but it will surely be a hit.

You can try different lengths by working out the second radius for a shorter shoulder-to-hem measurement. I recommend a light, drapey fabric such as a silk satin, if you go maxi.

MEASUREMENTS NEEDED

HORIZONTAL MEASUREMENTS (SEE PAGE 18)
Back • Across Front • Across Back • Bust
Underbust • Waist • Hip • Round Sleeve
Round Elbow • Wrist

VERTICAL MEASUREMENTS (SEE PAGE 19)
Shoulder to Across Front • Shoulder to Across Back
Shoulder to Bust • Shoulder to Underbust
Shoulder to Waist • Shoulder to Hip
Sleeve Length • Underarm Length • Elbow Length

OTHER MEASUREMENTS (SEE PAGE 19)
Apex • Flare length (see page 49)

BLOCKS NEEDED
Flare Block (see page 48) • Dress Block
(see page 34) • Sleeve Block (see page 56)

AMOUNT OF FABRIC NEEDED
You will need fabric that is at least 150 cm (60 in.) wide if you are going for the maxi length.

SKIRT
Width = second radius x 2
Length = second radius + 2.5 cm (1 in.)

BODICE
Width = Bust measurement + 50 cm (20 in.)
Length = Shoulder to Waist measurement + 2.5 cm (1 in.)

SLEEVES
Width = Round Sleeve x 2 + 5 cm (2 in.)
Length = Sleeve Length + 4 cm (1½ in.)

EXTRA FABRIC FOR ROULEAUX
1.5 m (60 in.)

MATERIALS AND EQUIPMENT NEEDED
Fabric (the fabric must measure at least 150 cm/ 60 in.) from selvedge to selvedge if you are going for the maxi length) • Iron-on interfacing
Sewing thread to match fabric • Fabric scissors
Straight ruler • Tape measure
Iron and ironing board • Fabric marker
Sewing machine • Overlocker (optional)
Pins • Large needle

PREPARE THE SKIRT

1 To work out your first radius, add 25 cm (10 in.) to your waist measurement, divide by 3.14, then round that figure down to the nearest whole or half number. Work out your second radius, following the instructions for the Flare Block on page 50. Again following the Flare Block instructions, fold the fabric, omitting the zip allowance fold. Mark the first and second radii, then cut along the marked radius lines, cutting through all layers. Do not cut along the bias fold: the skirt should be in one piece. Leave the excess fabric folded, as you will need it to make the rouleaux in Step 15.

PREPARE THE BODICE

2 Fold the bodice fabric in half across the width. Draw a straight line down the length, 12.5 cm (5 in.) from the unfolded edge. Line up the folded edge with the drawn line.

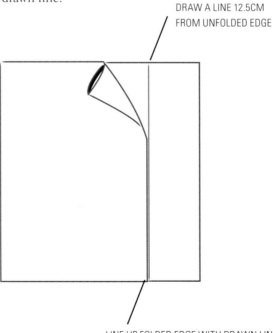

DRAW A LINE 12.5CM FROM UNFOLDED EDGE

LINE UP FOLDED EDGE WITH DRAWN LINE

3 Following Steps 3–12 of the Dress Block on pages 36–38, mark the vertical and horizontal measurements, subtracting 2.5 cm (1 in.) from the Shoulder to Waist measurement, which will be the seam line between the bodice and skirt. Cut around all the outer lines.

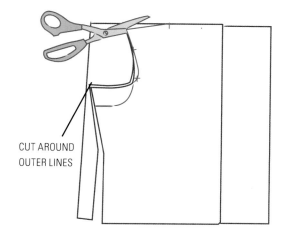

CUT AROUND
OUTER LINES

4 Separate the front from the back piece. Following Step 14 of the Dress Block, transfer the front armhole markings to the front piece and cut into the relevant lines for each piece.

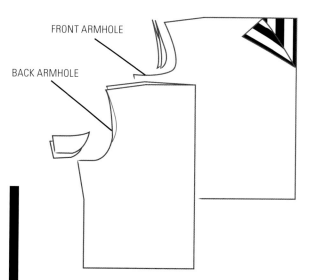

FRONT ARMHOLE

BACK ARMHOLE

5 Cut a shallow neckline in the back piece. (A standard neckline is 9 cm/ 3½ in. along the shoulder seam and 9 cm/ 3½ in. down the centre back; for this dress, I would suggest 9 cm/3½ in. along and only 4 cm/1½ in. down.)

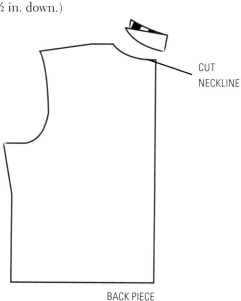

CUT
NECKLINE

BACK PIECE

6 Working on the front piece, with the piece still folded, measure down 2.5 cm (1 in.) from the inner shoulder. Starting from this 2.5-cm (1-in.) mark, measure the length from the inner shoulder seam to the waist minus 2.5 cm (1 in.) and then pivot and mark the Shoulder to Waist length at regular intervals from this point to the straight vertical edge of the fabric. This will form a curved line. Draw a straight line connecting the pivot point to the end of the curved line at the straight edge.

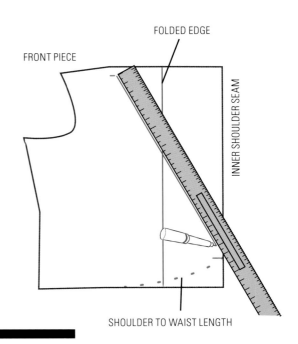

FRONT PIECE

FOLDED EDGE

INNER SHOULDER SEAM

SHOULDER TO WAIST LENGTH

CUT NOTCHES WHERE DRAWN LINE MEETS CUT EDGE

CENTRE FRONT

7 Cut along these lines and notch the top and bottom of the straight line drawn in step 2; this straight line represents the centre front.

8 With the pieces still folded, lay the back over the front, matching up the centres. Following Steps 15–22 of the Dress Block on pages 39–40, mark and sew the vertical and side bust darts and realign the front armholes.

9 For the waistband, from your extra fabric cut a strip 5 cm (2 in.) deep with a length of your Waist measurement plus 25 cm (10 in.). Cut a strip of interfacing the same size and fuse it to the wrong side of the fabric. Along both long edges, notch the centre of the strip and 12.5 cm (5 in.) in from each short edge.

10 Lay the front pieces over each other, right sides up, matching up the centre front notches. Pin a straight line from notch to notch.

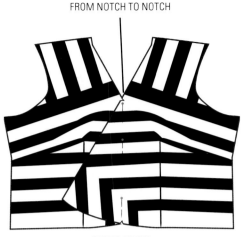

FRONT PIECES

ASSEMBLE THE BODICE

11 With right sides together, place the front pieces on the back piece. Sew the shoulder seams with a 1.2-cm (½-in.) seam allowance and the side seams with a 2-cm (¾-in.) seam allowance. Overlock or zig-zag stitch the seams.

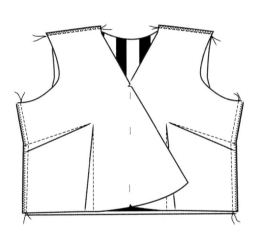

SEW WAISTBAND
TO SKIRT

SEW BODICE TO
WAISTBAND

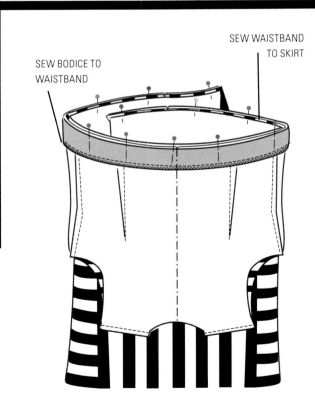

12 Unpin the front bodice sections. With right sides together, matching the centre back and notches, pin then sew the waistband to the waist of the bodice. Overlock or zig-zag stitch the seam. Matching up the centre back fold of the skirt with the centre back notch in the waistband, pin and sew the skirt to the bottom edge of the waistband in the same way, then overlock or zig-zag stitch the seam.

MAKE THE ROULEAUX

13 Now you need to make some rouleaux ties. Each one should be about 70cm (27 in.) long. Take the fabric left over from the skirt, which should be in one piece, and cut it in half, giving you a smaller piece to work with. Make a 90-degree fold by lining up the straight edges. Press. Draw a line parallel to the fold, 4 cm (1½ in.) from the fold. Cut along the line, then cut along the fold.

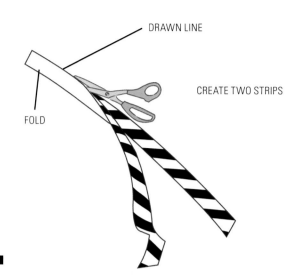

DRAWN LINE

CREATE TWO STRIPS

FOLD

14 Fold each strip in half, right sides together, and sew, taking a 6-mm (¼-in.) seam allowance. Thread a large needle, tie the end of the thread to the slanted ends of the rouleaux and push the blunt end of the needle all the way through. Pull gently on the needle to turn the rouleaux right side out. Knot the straight ends of the rouleaux to finish them off.

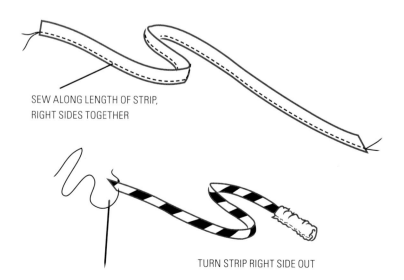

SEW ALONG LENGTH OF STRIP, RIGHT SIDES TOGETHER

TURN STRIP RIGHT SIDE OUT

NOTES
Some people press their rouleaux with the seam line in the centre of the back, so that it's not visible. I prefer not to press, as these rouleaux are so fine – I think it looks nice if they're not completely flat, but more 3-D, like small tubes.

15 Using the other half of the leftover fabric, repeat steps 13–14 to cut two more rouleaux, this time cutting them 10 cm (4 in.) wide and about 62 cm (24 in.) long. Sew the slanted ends shut and use a pen to turn them right side out. Set these wider strips aside. Overlock or zig-zag stitch the open ends of all four rouleaux.

16 Pin the overlocked end of one narrow rouleau to the inner side seam of the right front piece, just above the waistband. Pin the other narrow rouleau to the left front piece at the top edge of the waistband, on the right side of the garment. Stitch two lines of stitching across the ends of each rouleaux to secure them in place.

17 Stitch one wide rouleau to the edge of the right front piece at waist level, on the right side of the garment. Line up the overlocked edge of the other wide rouleau along the side seam of the left front piece, pointing towards the back piece. Sew across the rouleau 1.2 cm (½ in.) inside the overlocked edge.

SEW THE SECOND NARROW ROULEAU TO WRONG SIDE OF DRESS, AT SIDE SEAM

SEW THE FIRST NARROW ROULEAU TO WRONG SIDE OF LEFT DRESS FRONT PIECE

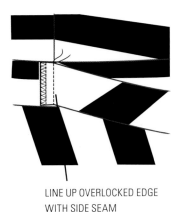

LINE UP OVERLOCKED EDGE WITH SIDE SEAM

18 Flip the rouleau back towards the front piece and sew across it again, 1.2 cm (½ in.) from the first seam, then sew a parallel line 3 mm (⅛ in.) inside the initial seam.

FLIP ROULEAU AND SEW
TWO PARALLEL LINES

HEM THE DRESS

19 From one front hem, overlock or zig-zag stitch along the edge, in one continuous flow, up the skirt edge, around the neckline, and down to the hem of the other front hem. Hem all around, using a narrow machine-rolled hem (see page 14).

MAKE AND SET IN THE SLEEVES

20 Following the instructions in the Sleeve Block (page 56), cut and set in two standard sleeves.

CROSS-FRONT TOP

NOTES

Always fold fabric right sides together unless otherwise stated. It is important to press every fold to create definite creases. Take a 1.2-cm (½-in.) seam allowance throughout unless otherwise stated.

S ometimes I want to look really smart without reaching for a conventional shirt (you've probably noticed that conventional and I don't always get along!). For this project I have used a white cotton shirting fabric; this is a play on the standard shirt. Team this look with some tapered or wide-leg trousers for office chic. And don't limit yourself to my fabric choice – how about some jazzy sequin fabric, for a completely different look?

MEASUREMENTS NEEDED

HORIZONTAL MEASUREMENTS (SEE PAGE 17)
Back • Across Front • Across Back • Bust
Underbust • Waist • Hip • Round Sleeve
Round Elbow • Wrist

VERTICAL MEASUREMENTS (SEE PAGE 17)
Shoulder to Across Front • Shoulder to Across Back
Shoulder to Bust • Shoulder to Underbust
Shoulder to Waist • Shoulder to Hip • Shoulder to Hem
Sleeve length • Underarm length • Elbow length

OTHER MEASUREMENTS (SEE PAGE 18)
Apex

BLOCK NEEDED
Dress Block (see page 34)
Sleeve Block (see page 56)

AMOUNT OF FABRIC NEEDED

BODICE FABRIC
Width = largest horizontal measurement + 56 cm (22 in.)
Length = shoulder to hem measurement + 5 cm (2 in.)

SLEEVE FABRIC
Width = Round Sleeve x 2 + 12.5 cm (5 in.)
Length = Sleeve Length + 4 cm (1½ in.)

EQUIPMENT NEEDED
Fabric • Bias binding • Invisible zip
Sewing thread to match fabric • Fabric scissors
Straight ruler • Tape measure • Iron and
ironing board • Fabric marker
Sewing machine • Pins • Invisible zip foot (optional)

1 The back and front will be cut separately. Cut your bodice fabric in half across the width. Fold one piece in half across the width again, then fold over and press a 2.5-cm (1-in.) zip allowance strip along the opposite edge, folding over both layers of fabric together; this fold is the centre back. The top edge is the shoulder seam and the bottom edge is the hem.

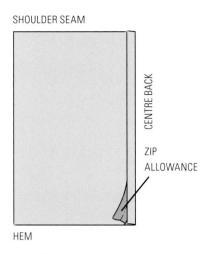

SHOULDER SEAM

CENTRE BACK

ZIP ALLOWANCE

HEM

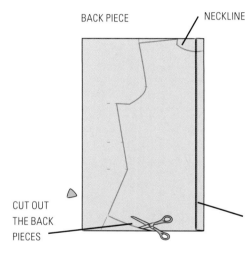

BACK PIECE

NECKLINE

CUT OUT THE BACK PIECES

ZIP ALLOWANCE

2 Following Steps 3–12 of the Dress Block mark your vertical and horizontal measurements on this back piece up to hip level (or your desired top Shoulder to Hem length) with the following changes: omit the front armhole and mark the neck hole 9 cm (3½ in.) along the shoulder seam and 4 cm (1½ in.) down the zip allowance fold. Draw the curved hem, following Step 8 of the Bodice Block (see page 28). Cut out and set aside.

3 Fold the rest of the bodice fabric in half across the width. Lay the cut-out back piece on top, lining up the zip allowance fold with the fold. Fold the back piece back along the Waist line. Draw a straight line parallel to the Waist line, 1.2 cm (½ in.) above the folded Waist line. Cut along this line.

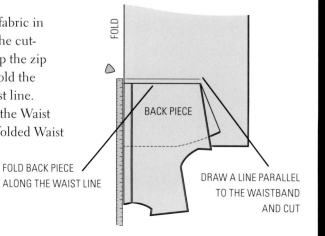

FOLD

BACK PIECE

FOLD BACK PIECE ALONG THE WAIST LINE

DRAW A LINE PARALLEL TO THE WAISTBAND AND CUT

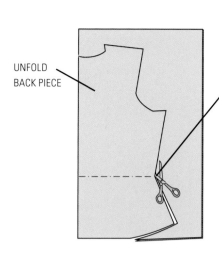

UNFOLD
BACK PIECE

CUT FRONT PIECE UP TO
WAIST LEVEL ONLY

4 Flip the back piece back so that the whole of the zip allowance fold is once more lined up with the fold on the front piece. Use the back piece as a template to cut around the hem and the side seam, up to the waist level. This is the bottom section of the front piece; set it aside.

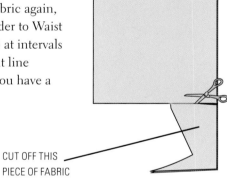

5 Working on the front piece fabric again, measure and mark the Shoulder to Waist measurement plus 1.2 cm (½ in.) at intervals from the top edge. Draw a straight line across the fabric and cut so that you have a levelled Waist line.

CUT OFF THIS
PIECE OF FABRIC

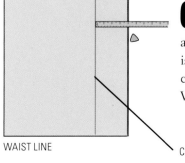

SHOULDER SEAM

WAIST LINE

CENTRE FRONT

6 Measure 10 cm (4 in.) from the open edge and draw a straight line running all the way down the fabric. The top edge is the shoulder seam, the line drawn is the centre front, and the bottom edge is the Waist line.

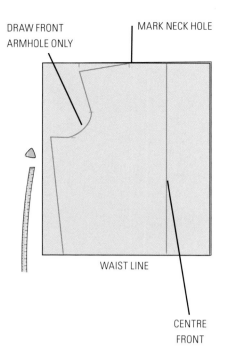

DRAW FRONT ARMHOLE ONLY

MARK NECK HOLE

WAIST LINE

CENTRE FRONT

7 Following Steps 3–12 of the Dress Block, measure and mark the vertical and horizontal measurements. Remember that this is the front section, so this time omit the back armhole, and mark the neck hole only on the shoulder seam, 9 cm (3½ in.) from the centre front line.

8 From the 9-cm (3½-in.) mark at the shoulder, measure down to the Waist plus 1.2 cm (½ in.). From this same point, pivot and mark the same length at regular intervals from this point to the vertical edge of the fabric. This will form a curved line. Draw a straight line that connects the shoulder mark to the end of the pivot mark. Cut along these lines and notch the centre line along the Waist line.

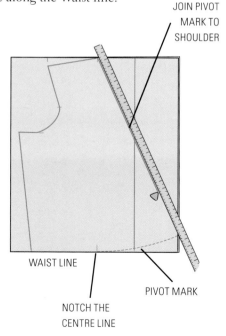

JOIN PIVOT MARK TO SHOULDER

WAIST LINE

NOTCH THE CENTRE LINE

PIVOT MARK

9 Arrange the front pieces as shown.

BOTTOM SECTION (THIS WAS CUT AND PUT ASIDE IN STEP 4)

10 Lay the back over the front, lining up the centre folds on the back with the line drawn on the centre front. Mark the vertical and side bust darts, following Steps 15–21 of the Dress Block. Remember, however, that there will be a seam along the Waist line in the front; when drawing your front vertical dart, be sure to accommodate this by drawing a straight 1.2-cm (½-in.) line over what will be the Waist line seam allowance.

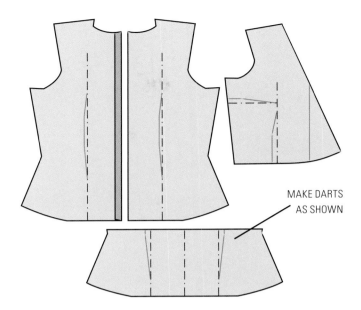

MAKE DARTS
AS SHOWN

11 Sew the darts in the front and back pieces and press the darts outwards. Be careful not to press out the centre creases in both the front and the back pieces.

12 Working on the back piece, sew down the zip allowance fold from the neckline for 7.5 cm (3 in.).

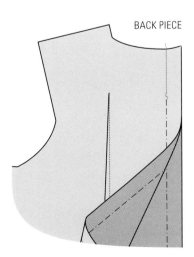

BACK PIECE

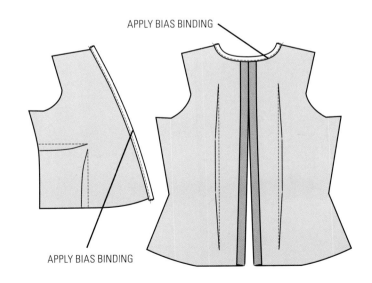

APPLY BIAS BINDING

APPLY BIAS BINDING

13 Apply ready-made bias binding to the back neckline and the centre front edges of the front piece (see page 13).

14 With both pieces right side up and matching up the notches, cross the right front piece over the left and pin together.

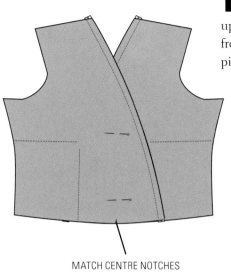

MATCH CENTRE NOTCHES

15 With right sides together, matching the notches to the centre fold of the front bottom section, pin and sew the bottom section along the waist. The front of your top should now be in one piece.

SEW CROSSED FRONT PIECES TO BOTTOM SECTION

INSERT INVISIBLE ZIP

BACK PIECE

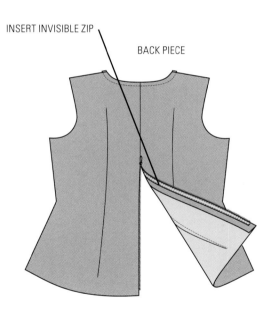

16 Insert an invisible zip (see page 15) into the open part of the back, inserting it upside down, as shown, and beginning 2.5 cm (1 in.) above the hemline. The zip pull should sit at the bottom edge of the fabric when the zip is closed.

17 With right sides together, place the front over the back, making sure that the centre front and centre back are lined up. Pin the sides. Working out from the centre, measure and mark your Bust divided by 4 along both side seams. Mark the Underbust, Waist and Hips in the same way, then join up the marks. Sew the side seams and the shoulder seams.

LINE UP CENTRE FRONT
AND CENTRE BACK

PLACE FRONT
OVER BACK

MARK SEAM ALLOWANCES
AND SEW SIDE SEAMS

18 Cut the sleeves, following Steps 1–7 of the Sleeve Block (pages 58–59). Set in the sleeves, following the instructions for a standard fitted sleeve head on page 60.

19 Hem the sleeves and top, using a rolled hem (see page 14).

NOTES

Always fold fabric right sides together unless otherwise stated. It is important to press every fold to create definite creases. Take a 1.2-cm (½in.) seam allowance throughout unless otherwise stated.

CHEVRON-PATTERNED COLLARLESS BLAZER

This project is one of those statement wardrobe pieces that you can throw on with a pair of jeans and tank top to really jazz up an otherwise dull outfit. Its clean lines and simple design make it a plain canvas for creativity. I have chosen a pop colour and a wax print to show the versatility of the garment. The print features a pattern of horizontal lines, which I made into a chevron effect. To achieve this without wasting too much fabric, I made a template out of poly-cotton. I strongly recommend having your chevrons pointing downwards, because this somehow makes the waist look smaller.

MEASUREMENTS NEEDED

HORIZONTAL MEASUREMENTS (SEE PAGE 18)
Back • Across Front • Across Back • Bust • Underbust
Waist • Hip • Round Sleeve • Round Elbow • Wrist

VERTICAL MEASUREMENTS (SEE PAGE 19)
Shoulder to Across Front • Shoulder to Across Back
Shoulder to Bust • Shoulder to Underbust
Shoulder to Waist • Shoulder to Hip
Sleeve Length • Underarm Length • Elbow Length

OTHER MEASUREMENTS (SEE PAGE 19)
Apex

BLOCKS NEEDED
Bodice Block (see page 24) • Sleeve Block (see page 56)

AMOUNT OF FABRIC NEEDED

POLY-COTTON
Width = largest horizontal measurement + 35 cm (14 in.)
Length = Shoulder to Hip measurement + 2.5 cm (1 in.)

JACKET FABRIC
Width = Hip measurement + 35 cm (14 in.)
Length = shoulder to hem measurement + 7.5 cm (3 in.)

LINING FABRIC
Width = Hip measurement + 35 cm (14 in.)
Length = shoulder to hem measurement + 7.5 cm (3 in.)

FOR SLEEVES
Width = Round Sleeve x 2 + 5 cm (2 in.)
Length = Sleeve Length plus 4 cm (1½ in.)

EQUIPMENT NEEDED
Poly-cotton • Fashion fabric • Lining fabric
Iron-on interfacing • Sewing thread to match fabric
Fabric scissors • Straight ruler • Tape measure
Iron and ironing board • Fabric marker
Sewing machine • Hand sewing needle • Pins

MAKING THE TEMPLATES

1 Fold the poly-cotton in half across the width. Draw a straight line down the length of the fabric, 2.5 cm (1 in.) from the edge opposite the fold. The top edge is the shoulder seam, the bottom edge is the hem and the drawn line is the centre front and back. Following Steps 3–12 of the Bodice Block on pages 26–29, measure and mark the vertical and horizontal measurements, including the inner edge of the neckline but omitting the neck hole.

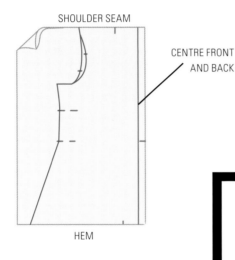

SHOULDER SEAM

CENTRE FRONT AND BACK

HEM

2 To create the back neck hole, measure and mark 4 cm (1½ in.) below the shoulder seam along the centre line. Draw a curve to the first mark along the shoulder seam (the inner edge of the neckline).

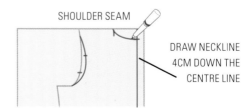

SHOULDER SEAM

DRAW NECKLINE 4CM DOWN THE CENTRE LINE

3 To create the front opening, measure and mark your Shoulder to Waist measurement plus 1.2 cm (½ in.) along the open edge. Draw a straight line that connects the shoulder seam to the marked point. Measure 5 cm (2 in.) out from the centre line and mark. Then draw a line that connects that mark to the mark along the open edge.

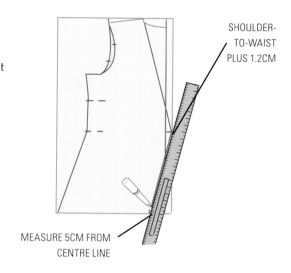

SHOULDER-TO-WAIST PLUS 1.2CM

MEASURE 5CM FROM CENTRE LINE

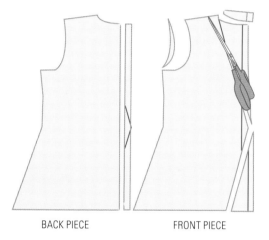

BACK PIECE   FRONT PIECE

4 Cut around all the outer markings, cutting through both layers. Then separate the two pieces and cut off the excess for each piece.

5 Use these templates to cut out your fashion fabric pieces; you do not need any extra seam allowances, so cut your fabric exactly to the template size.

CREATING THE CHEVRON PATTERN

6 Fold the fashion fabric in half along the length, right sides together, making sure that the pattern lines are well matched up. Pin your templates on the bias, so that the pattern lines run diagonally down the templates at an angle of 45°. Cut around your pieces, adding a 1.2-cm (½-in.) seam allowance along the centre back edge.

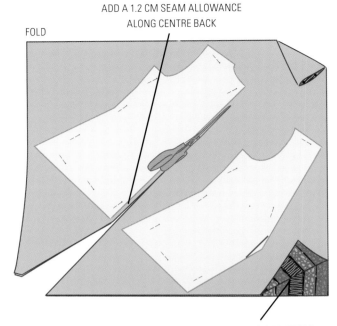

FOLD

ADD A 1.2 CM SEAM ALLOWANCE ALONG CENTRE BACK

MATCH STRIPES OF PATTERN

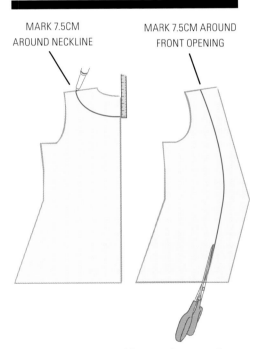

MARK 7.5CM AROUND NECKLINE

MARK 7.5CM AROUND FRONT OPENING

8 Lay your facing templates on fashion fabric (on the bias if you want to create the chevron effect) and cut around them, adding 1.2 cm (½ in.) along the cut edges and also at the centre back edge of the neck hole section. The rest of the templates will be used for the lining.

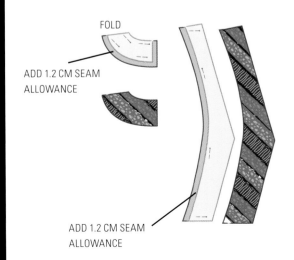

FOLD

ADD 1.2 CM SEAM ALLOWANCE

ADD 1.2 CM SEAM ALLOWANCE

7 To make the neckline and centre front facing templates, unpin the templates from the fashion fabric and mark a 7.5-cm (3-in.) border around the back neck hole and the front opening. N.B. On the front section, measure from the drawn centre front line, not from the tip of the cross-over section. Cut along these drawn lines.

166

CUTTING THE LINING

9 Fold the lining fabric in half across the width. Pin the templates on top, with the centre back on the fold. Cut around the pieces, adding 1.2 cm (½ in.) along the cut edge.

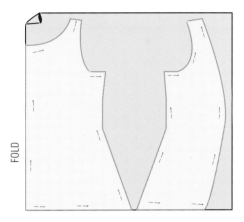

FOLD

10 Place the back fashion fabric pieces right sides together and sew the centre back seam. Press the seam open. Using the fashion fabric pieces as templates, cut out iron-on interfacing the same size and fuse it to the wrong side of the jacket pieces.

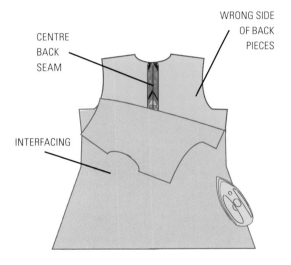

CENTRE BACK SEAM

WRONG SIDE OF BACK PIECES

INTERFACING

11 With right sides together, sew the facing pieces to the lining pieces, stitching along the lower edge of the back neckline and the inner edge of the centre front facings. Press the facings away from the lining pieces. Clip the lower edge of the neckline seam allowance.

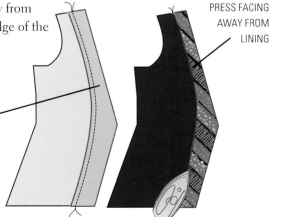

SEW FACINGS TO LINING

PRESS FACING AWAY FROM LINING

ASSEMBLING THE JACKET

12 Following Steps 15–24 of the Bodice Block (pages 30–32), mark and stitch the vertical and side bust darts. Repeat with the lining pieces.

PROJECT VARIATION

If matching up chevron stripes seems a little daunting, go for a solid colour. For the version pictured on page 163, I chose a bright yellow fabric, with a patterned lining, guaranteed to bring a pop of colour to any outfit!

13 With right sides together, lay the back lining over the back piece. Sew along the neckline and hem, then clip the neckline. Understitch the seams to the lining (see page 12) and press. Turn through so that the fashion fabric jacket and lining are wrong sides together.

14 With right sides together, lay the lining pieces over the corresponding front pieces. Sew along the centre front edge, then clip off the cross-over point at waist level. Understitch the seams to the linings and press. Turn through so that the fashion fabric jacket and lining are wrong sides together, then sew along the hem. Clip the corner. Understitch the seam to the lining and press.

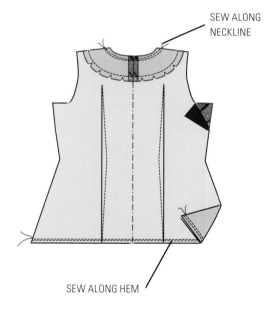

SEW ALONG NECKLINE

SEW ALONG HEM

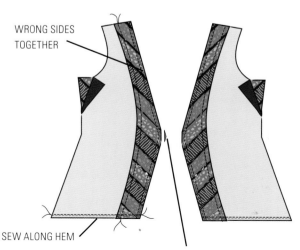

WRONG SIDES TOGETHER

SEW ALONG HEM

CLIP OFF CROSSOVER POINT

15 With right sides together, aligning the raw edges, lay the front jacket pieces over the back jacket piece. Tuck the lining pieces out of the way and sew the side seams of the fashion fabric only. Repeat with the lining, but leave a 15-cm (6-in.) gap in one on the side seams.

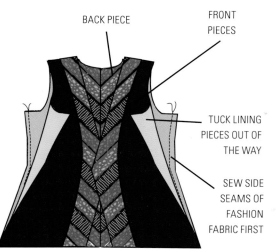

BACK PIECE

FRONT PIECES

TUCK LINING PIECES OUT OF THE WAY

SEW SIDE SEAMS OF FASHION FABRIC FIRST

16 Sew the shoulder seams from fashion fabric across to lining fabric. Snip into the seam joining the fashion fabric and lining to reduce bulk.

SEW ACROSS SHOULDER SEAM

17 Following the instructions for a Fitted Cap Sleeve (page 60), cut out a pair of fashion fabric sleeves and a pair of lining sleeves. Sew and set in the sleeves – lining sleeves to lining top and fashion fabric sleeves to fashion fabric top – following the instructions on page 60.

18 With right sides together, matching the side seams, sew the sleeve lining hem to the sleeve hem.

19 Turn the jacket right side out through the gap in the lining side seam. Test the fit and make any necessary adjustments. Once you are happy with the fit, slipstitch the gap closed.

ASYMMETRIC PEPLUM JACKET

T his is one of those jackets that is perfect to dress up or down – depending on your fabric and fit choice, you could wear this to work or for a night out. I love to look smart, but with my own spin on the norm; the collar in this jacket was a cut I stumbled on when I made a mistake with a past project – it was such a hit and has stuck with me since. I really hope you like it, too.

MEASUREMENTS NEEDED

HORIZONTAL MEASUREMENTS (SEE PAGE 18)

Back • Across Front • Across Back • Bust
Underbust Waist • Hip • Round Sleeve
Round Elbow • Wrist

VERTICAL MEASUREMENTS (SEE PAGE 19)

Shoulder to Across Front • Shoulder to Across Back
Shoulder to Bust • Shoulder to Underbust
Shoulder to Waist • Shoulder to Hip • Sleeve
Length • Underarm Length • Elbow Length

OTHER MEASUREMENTS (SEE PAGE 19)

Apex • Flare length (see page 49)

BLOCK NEEDED

Bodice Block (see page 24) • Full Flare Block
(see page 52) • Sleeve Block (see page 56)

AMOUNT OF FABRIC NEEDED

Width = second radius x 2 + 91.5 cm (1 yd)
Length = fabric that measures at least 145 cm (58 in.)
across from selvedge to selvedge

EQUIPMENT NEEDED

Fashion fabric • Lining fabric • Light or
medium weight iron-on interfacing • Sewing
thread to match fabric • Buttons • Fabric scissors
Straight ruler • Tape measure • Iron and ironing
board • Fabric marker • Sewing machine • Pins

NOTES

Always fold fabric right sides
together unless otherwise
stated. It is important to press
every fold to create definite
creases. Take a 1.2-cm (½-in.)
seam allowance throughout
unless otherwise stated.

CUTTING THE BODICE PIECES

1 Fold the fashion fabric, following Steps 1 and 2 of the Bodice Block on page 26. Following Steps 3–12 of the Bodice Block, measure and mark the vertical and horizontal measurements from shoulder down to Waist line level, omitting step 8. Flip the centre front fold out. Draw the neckline beyond the centre fold, angling downwards from the shoulder seam. Cut out the pieces, cutting along the back armhole markings, but do not cut the neckline.

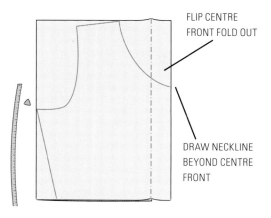

FLIP CENTRE FRONT FOLD OUT

DRAW NECKLINE BEYOND CENTRE FRONT

3 Using your fashion fabric pieces as a template, cut out lining and interfacing pieces for both front and back. Notch through the lining and dress fabric at the top and bottom of the fold in the front piece. This fold is the centre front. Fuse the interfacing to the wrong side of the fashion fabric pieces.

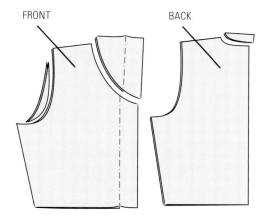

FRONT

BACK

2 Separate the front and back pieces. Cut along the front neckline and the front armhole. Draw a shallower neckline in the back and cut along the line.

4 Following Steps 15–24 of the Bodice Block (pages 30–32), mark and stitch the vertical and side bust darts in both the fashion fabric and the lining pieces. Set the bodice pieces aside.

MAKING THE PEPLUM

5 To make the peplum, add 7.5 cm (3 in.) to your Waist measurement. Work out your first radius (see page 49). With the first radius you will always get a decimal number; for this project you need to round it down to the nearest whole, ¼, ½, or ¾ place. Work out your second radius and add 10 cm (4 in.).

6 Following the instructions for the Full Flare on page 52, fold the peplum fabric in half and in half again along the fold, and press. Pivot and mark your second radius plus 5 cm (2 in.) at regular, close intervals. This should give you a smooth quarter-circle when the marks are joined up. Cut out, replicate the folding with lining fabric and use the already cut fashion fabric piece as a template to cut the lining.

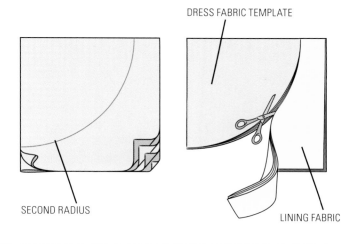

DRESS FABRIC TEMPLATE

SECOND RADIUS

LINING FABRIC

7 Working on the fashion fabric peplum, pick up the bottom edge of the top layer along the edge where the two folds are visible, move it up by 7.5 cm (3 in.) and press. Repeat with the lining.

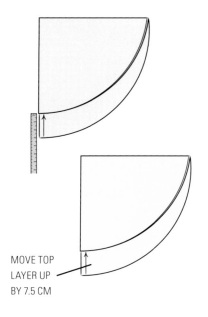

MOVE TOP LAYER UP BY 7.5 CM

8 Pivot and mark the first radius (see page 49) in the corner of the fashion fabric and lining peplums and cut. Cut open the shorter fold in both pieces. Set aside.

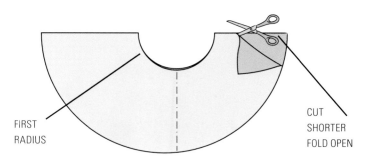

FIRST RADIUS

CUT SHORTER FOLD OPEN

CUTTING THE COLLAR PIECES

9 Take the bodice pieces and measure the combined length of the front and back necklines; this is the collar length. To cut the collar, take a piece of fabric that measures the collar length by 40.5 cm (16 in.) wide. Fold it in half along the length and notch the middle. Use the folded collar as a template to cut some interfacing, being careful not to cut into the folded edge. Fuse the interfacing to the wrong side of one half of the collar piece.

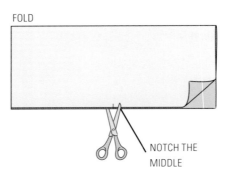

FOLD

NOTCH THE MIDDLE

10 Following the instructions for a Fitted Cap Sleeve (page 58), cut out a pair of fashion fabric sleeves, then use them as a template to cut a pair of lining sleeves.

ASSEMBLING THE BODICE

11 With right sides facing upwards, cross the left front bodice piece over the right front bodice along the centre front fold line and pin along the line.

PIN BODICE PIECES ALONG THE CENTRE FRONT LINE

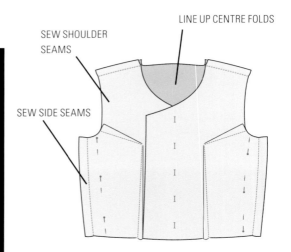

LINE UP CENTRE FOLDS

SEW SHOULDER SEAMS

SEW SIDE SEAMS

12 With right sides together, lay the front on top of the back piece, with the centre folds lined up. Pin and stitch the side and shoulder seams.

13 Unpin the centre front and check the fit. Make any necessary adjustments.

14 Copy the side and shoulder seam allowances to the bodice lining pieces and sew, leaving a 20-cm (8-in.) gap in one side seam.

15 Open up the peplum fashion fabric and lining circles and lay one on top of the other, right sides together. Sew around all the edges except the inner circle, taking a 1.5-cm (⅝ -in.) seam allowance. Snip off the corners and notch the circumference of the circle. Understitch the seam to the lining and press.

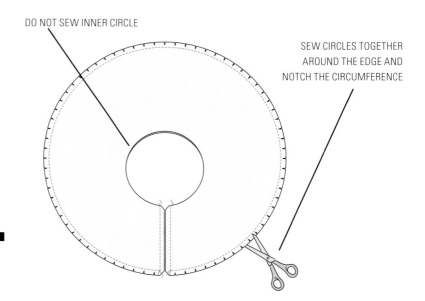

DO NOT SEW INNER CIRCLE

SEW CIRCLES TOGETHER AROUND THE EDGE AND NOTCH THE CIRCUMFERENCE

16 With right sides together, pin the centre back peplum to the centre back bodice, then pin the centre front of the peplum 1.2 cm (½ in.) inside the edge of the front bodice at each end. Pin the peplum all along the waist seam, easing it to fit as you go. Sew in place.

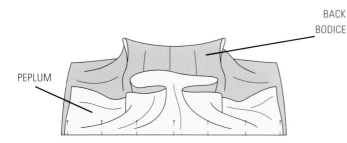

BACK BODICE

PEPLUM

NOTE
If you find that your peplum is too big to ease, make the excess fabric into a box pleat in the centre back as a design detail.

ATTACHING THE COLLAR AND SLEEVES

17 With right sides together, sew the shorter edges of the collar together and clip the corners. Turn right side out and press.

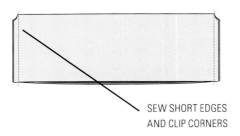

SEW SHORT EDGES AND CLIP CORNERS

19 Following the instructions on page 60, sew the sleeves and set them into the jacket and the lining.

ATTACHING THE LINING

20 Make sure that the sleeves are wrong side out on both lining and jacket. Lay the jacket down, right side up, and flip the peplum and collar back so that their seams are exposed.

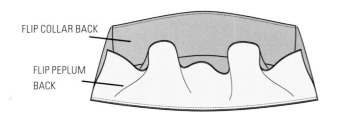

FLIP COLLAR BACK

FLIP PEPLUM BACK

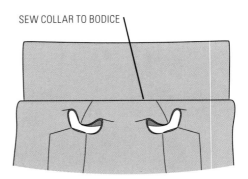

SEW COLLAR TO BODICE

18 With right sides together, taking a 1-cm (⅜-in.) seam allowance, sew the collar to the bodice neckline, starting and finishing your stitching 1.2 cm (½ in.) from the edge.

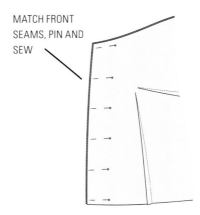

MATCH FRONT SEAMS, PIN AND SEW

21 Lay the lining over the jacket, right side down, matching up the front seams, and pin in place. Sew the lining to the jacket along the front seams, turn right side out and understitch the seam to the lining on both edges. Press.

22 Turn the jacket inside out again and match up the neckline and waist seams. Sew the seams and clip the corners.

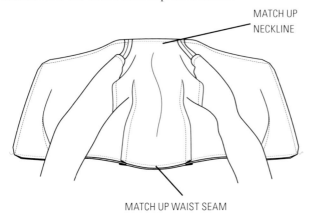

MATCH UP
NECKLINE

MATCH UP WAIST SEAM

23 With right sides together, matching the seams, sew the wrist of the sleeve and sleeve lining together.

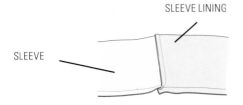

SLEEVE LINING

SLEEVE

24 Turn the jacket right side out through the gap in the lining side seam. Slipstitch the gap closed. Press the waist and neckline seams.

25 Use a sewing machine to create buttonholes 2 cm (¾ in.) inside the edge of the right centre front, then sew buttons to the left centre front to correspond.

PROJECT VARIATION

This version is made from a grey check wool to match the Pencil Skirt (see page 110). I have increased the sleeve head height to create dramatic puffed sleeves. See Sleeve Block on page 56 for more on different types of sleeve.

MERMAID-STYLE EVENING GOWN

NOTES

Always fold fabric right sides together unless otherwise stated. It is important to press every fold to create definite creases. Take a 1.2-cm (½-in.) seam allowance throughout unless otherwise stated.

MEASUREMENTS NEEDED

HORIZONTAL MEASUREMENTS (SEE PAGE 17)
Back • Across Front • Across Back • Bust • Underbust
Waist • Hip • Round Sleeve • Round Elbow • Wrist

VERTICAL MEASUREMENTS (SEE PAGE 17)
Shoulder to Across Front • Shoulder to Across Back
Shoulder to Bust • Shoulder to Underbust • Shoulder
to Waist • Shoulder to Hip • Shoulder to Hem Sleeve
Length • Underarm Length • Elbow Length

OTHER MEASUREMENTS (SEE PAGE 18)
Apex

BLOCK NEEDED
Dress Block (see page 34) • Sleeve Block (see page 56)

AMOUNT OF FABRIC NEEDED

DRESS FABRIC
5 times your shoulder to hem measurement

LINING FABRIC
Width = Hip measurement + 35.5 cm (14 in.)
Length = Overbust to Hem measurement + 2.5 cm (1 in.)

POLY-COTTON (FOR TEMPLATE)
Width = Hip measurement + 35.5 cm (14 in.) divided by 2
Length = shoulder to hem measurement

EQUIPMENT NEEDED
Poly-cotton or paper for template • Fashion fabric
Lining fabric • Plastic boning • Invisible zip
(see page 15) • Sewing thread to match fabric,
plus contrasting thread for tacking • Fabric scissors
Straight ruler • Tape measure • Iron and ironing board
Fabric marker • Sewing machine
Pins • Invisible zipper foot • Overlocker (optional)

When it comes to long gowns, my natural instinct is to go for a luscious mermaid cut, which I think is very versatile and feminine. It can be used for anything from a wedding gown, bridesmaid's dress, evening gala attire or a prom dress. Play with fabrics, embellishments and trims, as this will really make the dress your own.

MAKING THE TEMPLATES

1 I use poly-cotton to make my templates, but you can use paper if you prefer. Fold the template material in half across the width and press the fold. The fold is both centre front and centre back. Along the top edge, working out from the centre fold, measure and mark your Apex divided by 2.

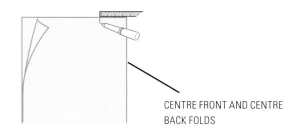

CENTRE FRONT AND CENTRE BACK FOLDS

2 Note your Shoulder to Overbust measurement minus 1.2 cm (½ in.), and place your tape measure on the top edge at this point. For instance, if your Shoulder to Overbust measurement is 15 cm (6 in.), then the 13.8-cm (5½-in.) mark on your tape measure will be level with the top edge of the template material. Keep your tape measure there and mark the following vertical measurements: 21.5 cm/8½ in. (this is your Bust line), Shoulder to Underbust, Shoulder to Waist, Shoulder to Hip, Shoulder to Knee.

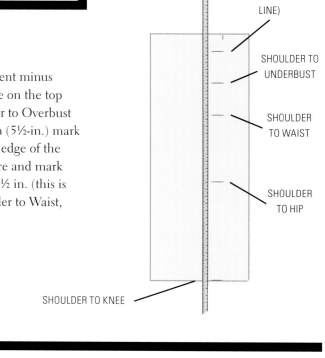

21.5 CM (BUST LINE)

SHOULDER TO UNDERBUST

SHOULDER TO WAIST

SHOULDER TO HIP

SHOULDER TO KNEE

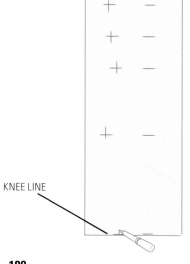

KNEE LINE

3 Along these reference points, mark with a small cross the corresponding horizontal measurements: Bust line and Hip divided by 4 plus 5 cm (2 in.); Waist and Underbust divided by 4 plus 7.5 cm (3 in.). At the Knee Line (the bottom edge), mark your Waist measurement divided by 4 plus 2.5 cm (1 in.).

4 From the cross at the Bust line, draw a straight 5-cm (2-in.) horizontal line back towards the centre fold. Then draw a diagonal line from the end of this straight line up to the mark made at the top edge. For the sweetheart neckline, from the mark at the top edge, draw a diagonal line that meets the centre fold about 10 cm (4 in.) below the top corner. (This depth is really up to you – you can make your sweetheart neckline as deep or as shallow as you like.)

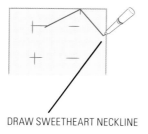

DRAW SWEETHEART NECKLINE

5 Join up all the crosses along the sides, making sure that the line around the hip area is rounded. Cut along your lines through all the layers, then notch the Underbust line, Waist line and Hip line. Separate the front from the back by cutting through the centre fold.

UNDERBUST LINE

WAIST LINE

HIP LINE

6 Working on the back piece, draw a concave arch from the inner end of the straight line at the bust level to 2.5 cm (1 in.) below the lowest point of the sweetheart neckline. (Again, you can make this point low as you like.) Cut along this line.

FRONT PIECE

BACK PIECE

LAY FRONT ON TOP OF BACK

FOLD MEETS POINT OF SWEETHEART NECKLINE

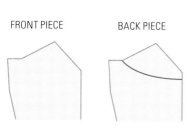

VERTICAL DART FOLD

7 Lay the front piece on top of the back piece again and make a vertical dart fold that is half your Apex measurement from the centre fold. Press this fold right down the length of the dress pieces. If you have placed this fold correctly, it should intercept the point of your sweetheart neckline.

8 Following Steps 20–21 of the Dress Block on page 40, mark the vertical darts, remembering always to draw the darts to the left of the dart crease. Do not mark the side bust darts yet. On the front piece, the bust dart will be at the peaks of the sweetheart neckline; the bust dart is 2.5 cm (1 in.) deep and 7.5 cm (3 in.) long, ending 6 mm (¼ in.) from the fold. At the waistline and underbust line levels the dart is 2.5 cm (1 in.) deep rather than the usual 1.2 cm (½ in.), so make marks that distance from the crease and join them with a straight line. Then from waistline level draw a line upwards that is 16.5 cm (6 ½ in.) long in total, passing through the underbust mark and then diagonally up to the dart crease, and another line 18 cm (7 in.) long down to touch the dart crease. On the back, the dart is 1.2 cm (½ in.) deep at the top edge.

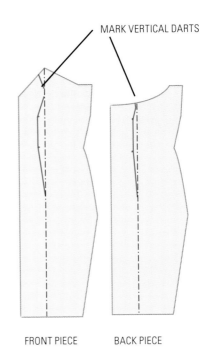

MARK VERTICAL DARTS

FRONT PIECE   BACK PIECE

NOTE

Don't worry if the edges don't match up at the sweetheart peak, or at the top of the back. When you have sewn your darts, simply push the dart seams towards the side seams and smooth out the sweetheart line.

9 Sew the darts in the front and back pieces. Note that the front dart is in two sections, but sewn as one continuous dart. Fold the fabric along the vertical crease. Start at the bust dart and, as you approach the end of the drawn line, keep sewing 6 mm (¼ in.) from the fold till you reach the other dart line. Press the darts towards the side seams.

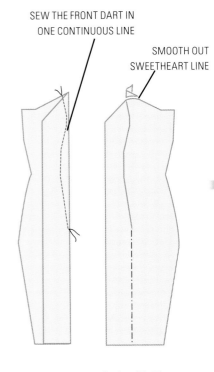

SEW THE FRONT DART IN ONE CONTINUOUS LINE

SMOOTH OUT SWEETHEART LINE

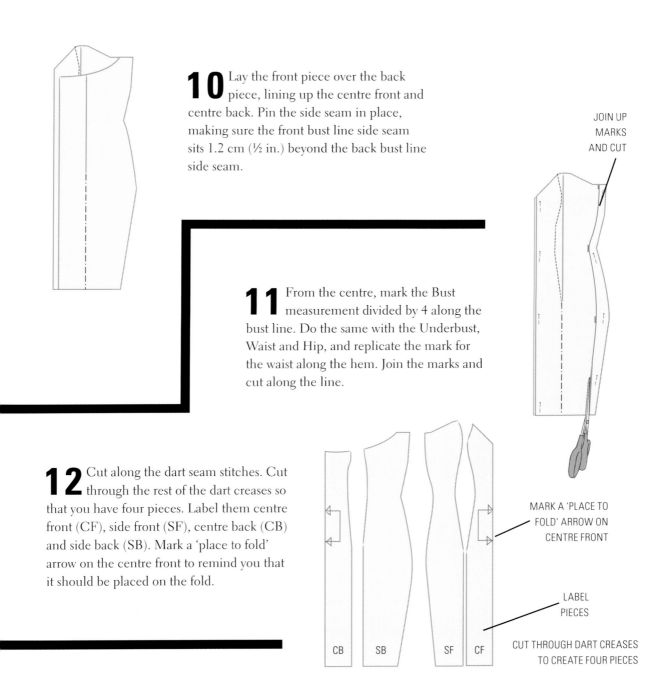

10 Lay the front piece over the back piece, lining up the centre front and centre back. Pin the side seam in place, making sure the front bust line side seam sits 1.2 cm (½ in.) beyond the back bust line side seam.

JOIN UP
MARKS
AND CUT

11 From the centre, mark the Bust measurement divided by 4 along the bust line. Do the same with the Underbust, Waist and Hip, and replicate the mark for the waist along the hem. Join the marks and cut along the line.

12 Cut along the dart seam stitches. Cut through the rest of the dart creases so that you have four pieces. Label them centre front (CF), side front (SF), centre back (CB) and side back (SB). Mark a 'place to fold' arrow on the centre front to remind you that it should be placed on the fold.

MARK A 'PLACE TO
FOLD' ARROW ON
CENTRE FRONT

LABEL
PIECES

CB SB SF CF

CUT THROUGH DART CREASES
TO CREATE FOUR PIECES

13 Work out what is missing from the dress length by subtracting your Shoulder to Knee measurement from the Shoulder to Floor measurement. If you will be wearing high heels with your dress, take this into account and add a little extra when measuring your Shoulder to Floor length. I think it's quite nice when mermaid gowns puddle a little bit, so if you wish to have this effect make it another 7.5 cm (3 in.) longer.

CUTTING THE FASHION FABRIC AND LINING PIECES

14 You are going to work with the fashion fabric in one long piece. Take one end of the fashion fabric, fold it in half lengthways so that the selvedges are touching and lay the centre front template on the fold. From the bottom edge of the template, mark the remaining length of the dress on the fabric at intervals, making the base a minimum of 2 times the width of the hem of the template. (You can extend beyond this – the more you extend, the more dramatic the mermaid cut will be.)

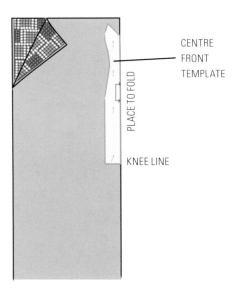

CENTRE
FRONT
TEMPLATE

PLACE TO FOLD

KNEE LINE

15 As you extend beyond the knee hem width, place the corner of your tape at the corner of the template's outer edge and pivot and mark the same length to however far you have decided to extend the base. From the knee line (the corner you just pivoted from), draw a straight diagonal line that joins to the extended bases.

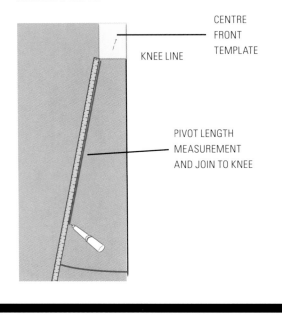

CENTRE
FRONT
TEMPLATE

KNEE LINE

PIVOT LENGTH
MEASUREMENT
AND JOIN TO KNEE

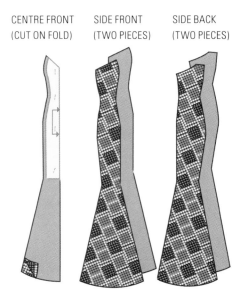

CENTRE FRONT
(CUT ON FOLD)

SIDE FRONT
(TWO PIECES)

SIDE BACK
(TWO PIECES)

16 Cut along your lines and template, adding a 1.2-cm (½-in.) seam allowance beyond the drawn diagonal line and the outer edge of the template. Do NOT add a seam allowance to the neckline or hem for any of the pieces. Do the same with the front side and back side pieces; remember, these are not on the fold – so place them in the middle of your folded dress fabric and repeat the base extension on either side of the knee line edge. Transfer your notches to the fashion fabric pieces.

17 For the back, fold the rest of the fabric in half along the selvedge. My dress features a small train, but you may want to omit this or extend it further. Lay the template in the middle of the fabric and extend the dart edge as far out as you wish. From the centre back edge, again extend as far out as you wish – but this time make the knee line to extension point 30.5 cm (12 in.) longer than it has previously been. When drawing the diagonal line in the centre back, start from 15 cm (6 in.) above the knee line and connect to the extension point.

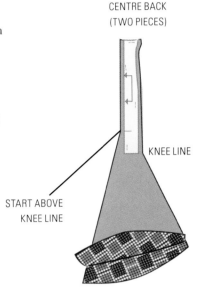

CENTRE BACK
(TWO PIECES)

KNEE LINE

START ABOVE
KNEE LINE

18 Use the templates to cut out your lining pieces. The lining does NOT extend beyond the knee. Do not forget to add a 1.2-cm (½-in.) seam allowance when cutting out, as in step 21.

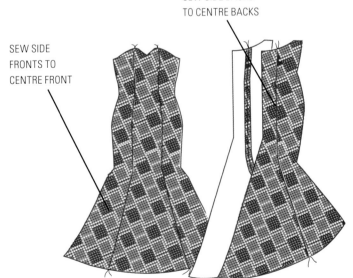

SEW SIDE BACKS
TO CENTRE BACKS

SEW SIDE
FRONTS TO
CENTRE FRONT

ASSEMBLING THE DRESS

19 With right sides together, sew the front side panels to either side of the centre front and the back side panels to the outer edges of the centre back pieces. Press the seams open. Repeat with the lining pieces.

INSERTING THE BONING

We will be inserting boning into the front and back dart lines on the lining fabric. Usually, boning is also inserted into the side panels and down to the lower abdomen, but I find that very uncomfortable so I am showing how to put it into the darts and only to waist level.

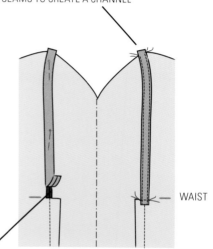

LINE UP BIAS BINDING OVER DART SEAMS TO CREATE A CHANNEL

20 Mark the Waist line on the wrong side of all the lining pieces. Trim the dart seams down to 6 mm (¼ in.) from the waist up, and press the seams open. Line the centre of the bias binding over the seam line and sew down either side of the binding to create a channel. This should only go down 1.2 cm (½ in.) below the Waist line. Sew across the base of the boning channels, directly on the Waist line.

TRIM DART SEAMS AND PRESS OPEN

WAIST

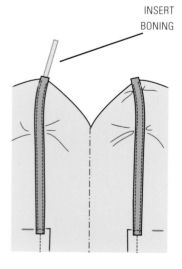

INSERT BONING

21 Insert the boning into the channels, cutting them 1.2 cm (½ in.) shorter than the length of the channel. Plastic boning is always curved because it is usually on a roll, so make sure that the curve is in correspondence to the section it is inserted into.

ASSEMBLING THE DRESS

22 Following the instructions on page 15, insert an invisible zip into the centre back of the fashion fabric pieces.

23 With right sides together, lay the dress front over the dress back and sew the side seams. Repeat with the lining pieces.

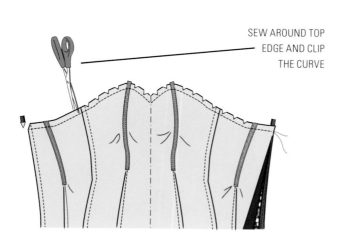

SEW AROUND TOP EDGE AND CLIP THE CURVE

24 Lay the lining over the dress, matching up the neckline and the seams. Sew around the top edge, then clip the curve. Understitch the seam to the lining (see page 12).

25 With right sides together, sew the lining and dress fabric together along the centre back seam, behind the teeth of the zip. Clip the top corner of the zip head to reduce the bulk.

26 Continue the lining centre back seam, stopping about 15 cm (6 in.) above the hem. Zig-zag stitch or overlock the unsewn section of the lining centre back seam.

27 Overlock the hem of the lining or hem with a machine-rolled hem (see page 14). Hem the dress with a machine-rolled hem.

First published in the United Kingdom in 2015 by
Pavilion
1 Gower Street
London
WC1E 6HD

ISBN 978-1-91049-614-5

A CIP catalogue record for this book is available from
the British Library.

10 9 8 7 6 5 4 3 2 1

Reproduction by COLOURDEPTH
Printed and bound by 1010 Printing International Ltd, China

This book can be ordered direct from the publisher at
www.pavilionbooks.com

Join the conversation online and share your creations
#FreehandFashion

PUBLISHERS' THANKS

We would like to thank Cloth House
(www.clothhouse.com) for supplying the beautiful
fabric used to make the cream peplum jacket, grey
peplum jacket and grey pencil skirt. Thanks also to
Hardwicks, London, for supplying the print fabric
for the mermaid dress. Thank you to our brilliant
models: Jemilla King, Anita Jones and Lucy Bradley.
Thanks to stylist Sandra Aji, photographers Laura
Lewis and Claire Pepper, illustrators Kate Simunek
and Stephen Dew, editors Sarah Hoggett and
Kate Haxell and designer Claire Clewley for her
assistance with the layout.

Illustrations: Kate Simunek and Stephen Dew.
All photography by Claire Pepper apart from
images on pages 66, 67 and 73, by Laura Lewis.

AUTHOR THANKS

First, I thank God for making all this possible.
I thank my husband for the invaluable support
throughout, and my parents and siblings for
always being there in all ways imaginable.
Thank you to my wonderful agent, Stuart
Cooper from Metrostar. A massive thanks
to everyone who worked on the book, to the
fabulous staff at Pavilion – most especially
Amy Christian and Zoë Anspach – Sarah
Hoggett, Kate Haxell, Sandra Aji, all the
models, photographers, and illustrators – you
guys are the best. And a big thanks to all
who have supported my journey since the
Sewing Bee! I thank you all.

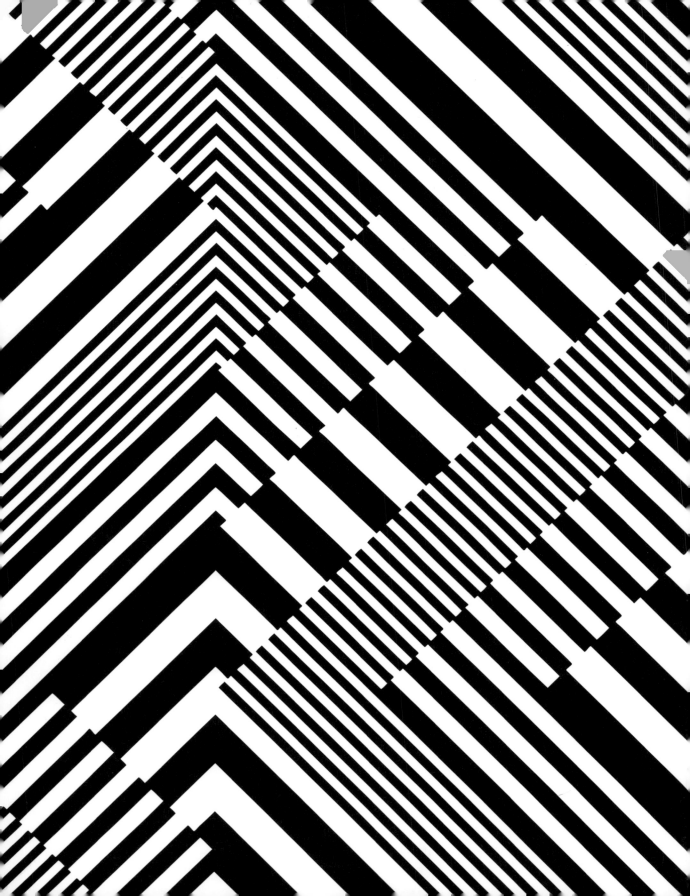

Community Learning & Libraries
Cymuned Ddysgu a Llyfrgelloedd

This item should be returned or renewed by the last date stamped below.

To renew visit:

www.newport.gov.uk/libraries